# Grade K

by Beverly Warkulwiz

Carson-Dellosa Publishing LLC
Greensboro, North Carolina

**Caution:** Before beginning any nature activity, ask families' permission and inquire about students' plant and animal allergies. Remind students not to touch plants or animals during the activity without adult supervision.

# Credits

Content Editor: Amy R. Gamble
Copy Editor: Julie B. Killian
Layout Design: Van Harris
Cover Design: Lori Jackson

This book has been correlated to state, common core state, national, and Canadian provincial standards. Visit *www.carsondellosa.com* to search for and view its correlations to your standards.

Carson-Dellosa Publishing LLC
PO Box 35665
Greensboro, NC 27425 USA
www.carsondellosa.com

ISBN 978-1-60996-467-2
03-119131151

# Table of Contents

# Skills Matrix

| Page Numbers | Number sense | Foundation of basic operations | Skip counting | Place value to tens | Sorting and classifying | Patterns | Algebra concepts | Measurement | Concepts of time | Geometry | Data analysis | Graphing | Probability | Problem solving |
|---|---|---|---|---|---|---|---|---|---|---|---|---|---|---|
| 6–9 | ● | | | | | | | | | | | | | |
| 10–13 | ● | | | | | | | | | | | | | ● |
| 14–17 | ● | | | | | | | | | | | | | ● |
| 18–21 | ● | ● | | | | | | | | | | | | ● |
| 22–25 | ● | ● | | | | | | | | | | | | ● |
| 26–29 | ● | ● | ● | | | | | | | | | | | ● |
| 30–33 | ● | ● | | | | | | | | | | | | ● |
| 34–37 | ● | | | ● | | | | | | | | | | |
| 38–41 | | | ● | | ● | | ● | | | ● | | | | ● |
| 42–45 | | | | | ● | ● | ● | | | ● | | | | ● |
| 46–49 | ● | ● | ● | | ● | ● | ● | | | ● | | | | ● |
| 50–53 | ● | ● | ● | | | ● | ● | | | | | | | ● |
| 54–57 | | | | | ● | | | ● | | | | | | ● |
| 58–61 | | | | | ● | | | ● | | | | | | ● |
| 62–65 | | | | | ● | ● | | ● | ● | | | | | ● |
| 66–69 | | | | | ● | | | ● | ● | | | | | ● |
| 70–73 | | | | | ● | | | | | ● | | | | ● |
| 74–77 | ● | | | | ● | | | | | ● | | | | ● |
| 78–81 | | | | | | | | | | ● | | | | ● |
| 82–85 | | | | | ● | | | | | | ● | ● | | ● |
| 86–89 | | | | | | | | | | | ● | ● | | ● |
| 90–93 | ● | | | | | | | | | | | | ● | ● |

CD-104541  © Carson-Dellosa

# Introduction

Kindergarten is likely one of the most difficult grades to teach. Children come to the kindergarten classroom with a variety of learning experiences, whether from home or preschool, and little or no information is often shared with you before the first day of school. For some students, the kindergarten curriculum will pose a significant challenge, while other students may have already mastered kindergarten skills and concepts. As you are expected to guide each student toward standards proficiency while differentiating the curriculum, doing so presents quite a challenge when teaching children in their first formal year of schooling.

You may already be familiar with the concept of guided reading: assessing students to determine their instructional reading levels and placing students in small, flexible groups based on those levels. In these small groups, teachers are better able to support students as they progress through a continuum of literacy skills.

Guided math is fashioned along the same lines. Before beginning a new skill or concept, you will assess students to discover what they have already mastered and what they still need to learn. You will then use this information to place students in small, differentiated groups. These small groups will provide an avenue for balanced and more individualized instruction. All students will be able to explore the same basic mathematical skills and concepts through activities that are tiered to meet their needs.

*Guided Math Made Easy* parallels the National Council of Teachers of Mathematics (NCTM) content strands: Number and Operations, Algebra, Measurement, Geometry, and Data Analysis & Probability. The lessons and activities included in this book are designed to reinforce or enrich specific objectives from each of the five content strands.

For each objective, you will find a teacher resource page and three activity sheets. The resource page includes one mini-lesson and three small-group lessons. The mini-lessons are intended for whole-group instruction to set the stage for the skills or the concepts to be explored through the identified objectives. The small-group lessons reflect three tiers of readiness: below grade level, on grade level, and above grade level. These hands-on small-group lessons will allow you to differentiate instruction to meet your students' needs. The activity sheets are also tiered to meet the needs of below-, on-, and above-grade-level learners. The activities can be used within the small-group lesson as guided practice, sent home as independent practice, placed at a math center as a review, or used as informal assessments.

We are confident that you will discover numerous opportunities for integrating the lessons and the activities presented in *Guided Math Made Easy* into your kindergarten math curriculum.

## Key

Below Level: ◯

On Level: ☐

Above Level: △

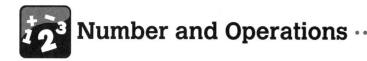

# Number and Operations

**Materials:**
- Several sets of number cards 1–10
- Linking cubes
- Tray or plastic tub
- Activity sheets (pages 7–9)

## Objective
Demonstrate relationships between numbers and quantities.

## Mini-Lesson

1. Invite 5 volunteers to line up at the front of the room. Have the remaining students count the volunteers as you touch each student's head. Write 5 on the board. Ask, "If we rearrange them, will there still be 5 students?" Encourage students to explain their reasoning.
2. Ask the volunteers to stand in a different order. Count again. Discuss the results. (The order of the students does not change the quantity.)
3. Give each student a set of 5 linking cubes.
4. Ask, "How many cubes do you have?" Have students point to each cube as they count, mix the cubes, and count again. If students miscount, encourage them to link the cubes as they count so that they do not "double count." Ask students to explain why lining up the cubes makes them easier to count.

## Group 1 ◯

**Counting Objects in a Set**

1. Give each student a set of 7 linking cubes. Ask, "How many cubes do you have?" Have students link their cubes and point to each cube as they count. Have them mix, link, and count again.
2. Display a number card and read the number to the group. Ask students to show that number by linking the cubes. Have students point and count aloud to check for accuracy. Repeat for each number.
3. Have each student show any number of cubes from 1 to 7 and then select the number card that matches his set. Repeat if time allows.
4. Ask students to share something they know about counting. Use the discussion as an opportunity to reinforce that the order of the objects does not change the quantity.

## Group 2 ☐

**Matching Sets and Numerals**

1. Give each student a set of 10 linking cubes. Ask, "How many cubes do you have?" Observe counting strategies and help as necessary.
2. Display a number card and ask students to identify the number. Have students show that number with their cubes (linked or unlinked). Repeat for each number from 1 to 10. If students miscount, encourage them to link the cubes so that they do not "double count."
3. Lay the cards facedown on the table. Have each student show any number of cubes from 1 to 10 and then flip over a card. If the number on the card matches the student's cubes, the card stays faceup. If not, the student flips the card back over. Have students take turns until all of the cards are faceup.

## Group 3 △

**Building Sets**

1. Give each student a set of 12 linking cubes and a set of number cards.
2. Say any number from 1 to 10. Have students show that number using the cubes and then label with the correct number card. Repeat for each number from 1 to 10.
3. Place all cubes on a tray or in a plastic tub and collect the cards. Shuffle 2 to 3 sets of cards and place them facedown on the table.
4. Have students take turns drawing the top card and gathering that number of cubes from the tray. If a student draws a card and enough cubes are not left on the tray or the tub, it is the next student's turn. Continue until all of the cards or the cubes are gone.
5. Challenge students to count their cubes at the end of the game.

Name_____

# Count the cubes. Circle the number of cubes in each set.

   1    2    3

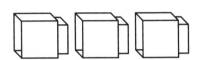   2    3    4

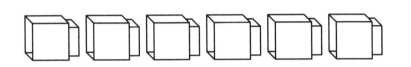   4    5    6

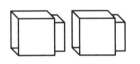   1    2    3

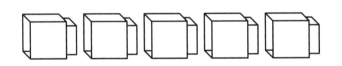   3    4    5

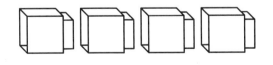   4    5    6

   5    6    7

Name_____

# Write the number of cubes in each set.

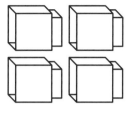

_____

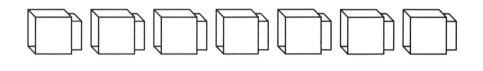

_____

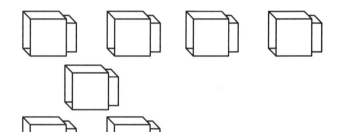

_____

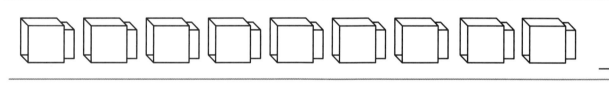

_____

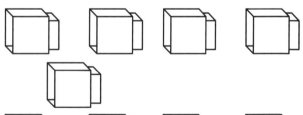

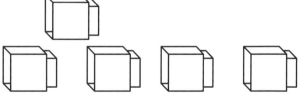

_____

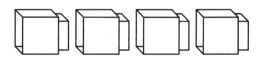

_____

Color the sets with the same number of cubes the same color.

**8**

Name_____

## Write the number of cubes in each set.

▢▢▢                                                    _____

▢▢▢▢▢▢▢▢                                    _____

▢▢▢▢▢▢▢▢▢                              _____

Color 12 cubes red. Color the rest of the cubes blue.
How many cubes are blue?

▢▢▢▢▢
▢▢▢▢▢          Number of blue cubes _____
▢▢▢▢▢
▢▢▢▢▢

Draw more than 7 cubes.

┌─────────────────────────────────┐
│                                 │
│                                 │
│                                 │
│                                 │
└─────────────────────────────────┘

How many cubes did you draw? _____

# Number and Operations

## Objective
Compare sets and determine how to make them equal.

**Materials:**
- Small paper plates
- Counting chips
- 6- and 10-sided dice
- Math journals
- Activity sheets (pages 11–13)

## Mini-Lesson

1. Invite 4 students to stand as a group on one side of the classroom and 6 students to stand on the other side.
2. Have the remaining students count the students in each group and determine which group has more and which has fewer.
3. Ask, "How many more students do we need to add to this group (with 4) to make the 2 groups equal, or the same?" Share answers and test predictions. Count to check.
4. Next, call up a group of 5 students and a group of 2 students. Have the remaining students count and compare to determine which group has more and which has fewer.
5. Ask, "How many students from this group (with 5) should sit to make the 2 groups equal?" Share answers and test predictions. Count to check.

## Group 1 ◯

**More or Less**
1. Give each student 2 small paper plates and 12 counting chips.
2. Instruct students to place ___ chips (0–6) on one plate and ___ chips on the other.
3. Ask, "Which plate has more chips?" or "Which plate has fewer chips?" Have students share their answers with the group.
4. Ask, "How many more chips should we add to this plate to make them equal?" Share answers and test predictions together. Count to check.
5. Repeat steps 2 to 4 several times with different numbers.
6. Have students explain more, fewer, and equal in their own words in their math journals.

## Group 2 ☐

**Add to Create Equality**
1. Give each student 2 small paper plates, 12 counting chips, and a 6-sided die.
2. Have students place any number of chips on one of their plates. Roll a die and ask students to tell you if they have more or fewer chips than the number rolled.
3. Model rolling the die and placing that number of chips on one plate. Roll again and place that number of chips on the other plate. Determine how many more chips you need to add to the plate with fewer chips to make the groups equal.
4. As students are working, ask, "Which plate has more and which has fewer?" or "How do you know that the number of chips is equal?"
5. Have students describe an example from the activity in their math journals.

## Group 3 △

**Subtract to Create Equality**
1. Give each student 2 paper plates, 18 counting chips, and a 10-sided die.
2. Follow step 3 from Group 2's lesson with a 10-sided die.
3. After students have mastered determining how many more, challenge them to determine how many chips they need to take away from the plate with more chips to make the groups equal.
4. Have students place any number of chips (up to 18) on one of their plates. Roll the die and ask students to determine how many more or fewer chips they need to equal the number rolled.
5. Encourage students to think aloud as they work and record their thought processes in their math journals.

Name_____

Use counting chips to answer the questions.
Circle your answers.

Which is more? 3 or 5      Which is less? 2 or 3

Which is more? 4 or 1      Which is less? 1 or 5

Circle the set that shows more than 3 dogs.

Circle the set that shows less than 3 cats.

How many more kids does one group need to make
the groups equal?

The group needs _____ more kids.

Name_____

Circle the set that shows more.

Circle the set that shows less.

 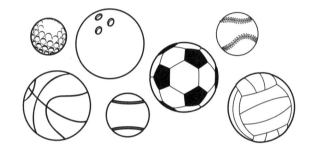

Draw a set of circles that is more than 5.


Draw a set of circles that is less than 5.


How many more kids does one group need to make the groups equal?

The group needs _____ more kids.

12

Name_____

Imagine that these are your balloons. Use the picture to answer the questions.

How many more balloons would you need
to have 12? _____

Maria has 6 balloons. Does she have more or less
than you? _____

How many balloons would you have to
give to Maria for both of you to have the
same number of balloons? _____

Count the circles. Draw a set of circles that has less
and a set that has more.

| Less | Count | More |
|---|---|---|
| How many circles? | How many circles? | How many circles? |
| _____ | _____ | _____ |

Circle the correct answers.

Which numbers are less than 5?    2    8    3    6

Which numbers are more than 7?    4    10    9    5

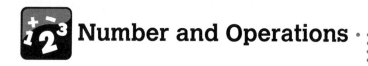

# Number and Operations

## Objective
Use ordinal numbers to problem solve.

**Materials:**
- Ordinal number signs (1st/first–5th/fifth)
- Ordinal number lines (1st–5th, 1st–10th, 1st–12th)
- Counting chips in various colors
- Index cards
- Activity sheets (pages 15–17)

## Mini-Lesson

1. Tape ordinal number signs in order on the board or on a wall. Select 5 students and have them stand off to the side.
2. Give clues to help the class determine which student should stand in which position. For example, "The first person should be a boy with glasses. The fifth person should be a girl with white sneakers."
3. Once students are in place, ask the class questions about the 5 students. For example, "Is the second person a boy or a girl?" or "Which person is wearing white sneakers?" Students should answer with ordinal numbers.
4. Repeat the process with another group of 5 students.
5. Then, challenge students to think of real-world situations where they would use ordinal numbers.

## Group 1 ◯

**Ordinal Position**
1. Give each student an ordinal number line (1st–5th) and 5 counting chips (each a different color).
2. Give simple directions. Tell students where to place each colored chip on the number line. For example, "The 3rd chip is blue. The 1st chip is red." Once students have placed all of the chips, have students clear their number lines.
3. Have students take turns being the "color caller." Have the first caller secretly place her chips on her number line and then give directions so that the remaining students can place their chips in the same order. Once students have placed all of their chips, have the caller reveal the order of her chips.
4. Repeat until every student has had a chance to be the caller.

## Group 2 ▢

**Matching Ordinal Numbers**
1. Write ordinal numbers (1st–10th) and ordinal number words (first–tenth) on index cards. Shuffle the cards and place them facedown on the table in a 3 x 4 array.
2. Give each student an ordinal number line (1st–10th) and 10 counting chips.
3. As a whole-class activity, have students take turns flipping over 2 cards at a time. If the cards match (for example, 1st and first), have students place chips on their number lines in the appropriate spaces and flip the cards back over. If chips are already on those spaces, have students remove the chips and then flip the cards back over. If the cards flipped do not match, simply have students flip the cards back over.
4. Have students continue until all of the spaces on their number lines are filled.

## Group 3 △

**Number Order**
1. Write ordinal number words (first–twelfth) on index cards. Shuffle the cards and place them facedown on the table.
2. Check for understanding by saying an ordinal number and having students touch the correct place on ordinal number lines (1st–12th).
3. Have students take turns choosing 1 card and placing it on the table in relationship to the other turned-over cards so that all of the cards will eventually be laid in order. For example, if fourth is already on the table, and a student chooses eighth next, she should place eighth to the right of fourth with some space between.
4. Have students continue until all of the cards are faceup in order on the table. Repeat with ordinal number cards (1st–12th).

Name_____

## Circle the 3rd animal.

## Circle the 1st student in line.

## Color the 4th shape green.

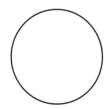   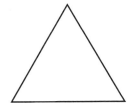

## Color the 2nd smiley face yellow.

## In which position is the ☐?    1st    2nd    3rd    4th

 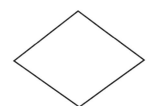 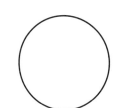 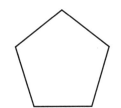

Name_____

Circle the 2nd animal. Draw a square around the 4th animal.

Color the first shape red. Color the sixth shape blue.

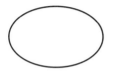      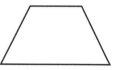

Circle the positions of the ovals.

1st  2nd  3rd  4th  5th 6th  7th  8th  9th

Follow the directions to draw shapes in the correct order.

Draw a circle in the 2nd box.

Draw a rectangle in the third box.

Draw an oval in the 5th box.

Draw a triangle in the 1st box.

Draw a square in the fourth box.

Name_____

# Follow the directions to see the secret message.

- Write H on the fourth line.
- Write F on the seventh line.
- Write M on the first line.
- Write U on the eighth line.
- Write I on the fifth line.

- Write A on the second line.
- Write N on the ninth line.
- Write T on the third line.
- Write S on the sixth line.
- Write ! on the tenth line.

___  ___  ___  ___  ___     ___  ___  ___     ___  ___

# Follow the directions to solve the riddle.
I can fly, but I am not a bird. I am colorful. What am I?

- Write B on the 2nd line.
- Write Y on the 10th line.
- Write E on the 6th line.
- Write F on the 8th line.
- Write U on the 3rd line.

- Write A on the 1st line.
- Write T on the 5th line.
- Write R on the 7th line.
- Write L on the 9th line.
- Write T on the 4th line.

___     ___  ___  ___  ___  ___  ___  ___  ___  ___

**Materials:**
- Overhead projector
- Counting chips
- Linking cubes
- Chart paper
- Math journals
- Blank 9 x 9 charts
- Activity sheets (pages 19–21)

## Objective
Combine or add to get more.

## Mini-Lesson

1. Use the overhead projector to demonstrate combining to get more. Place 2 counting chips on the left of the projector and 2 on the right. Have students count each set with you.
2. Say, "I wonder how many chips I will have if I put the sets of chips together." Then, move the chips to the center of the projector and count again. Recap what you did by saying, "I had 2 chips over here and 2 over here, but now I have 4 chips altogether."
3. Follow the same steps with 3 chips on the left and 3 chips on the right; 2 chips on the left and 3 chips on the right; and then 5 chips on the left and 2 chips on the right.
4. Use the words *add*, *more*, *in all*, and *altogether* as you work through each example.
5. Ask, "What happens when I put things together? (You get more.)

## Group 1 ○

**Combining Sets**
1. Give each student 12 linking cubes (6 of one color and 6 of another).
2. Guide students through the process of combining cubes to make sums to 7. For example, "If I have 1 red cube, and I add 3 blue cubes, I have 4 cubes." Also be sure that each value is represented by a different color.
3. Allow students time to explore this concept independently and encourage them to think aloud as they work. Ask questions such as, "How did you make 3?"
4. Challenge students to think of at least 2 different ways to make 4, 5, 6, and 7. Have students show and explain what they did with the cubes, then record their discoveries in their math journals.

## Group 2 ☐

**Combinations for Specific Sums**
1. Give each student 20 linking cubes (10 of one color and 10 of another).
2. Guide students through the process of combining cubes to show sums to 10. (See step 2 in the Group 1 lesson for an example of what to say.)
3. Allow students time to explore this concept independently and encourage them to think aloud as they work. Ask questions such as, "How did you make 7?"
4. Work together to find all of the combinations for 10 and record them on chart paper. Introduce how to read and write addition equations (for example, $3 + 7 = 10$).
5. Challenge students to think of at least 3 different ways to make 6, 7, 8, and 9. Have students record the equations for each combination in their math journals.

## Group 3 △

**Commutative Property**
1. Follow steps 1 to 3 in Group 2's lesson to introduce the concept.
2. Give each student a blank 9 x 9 chart. Have students number the left-column spaces 2 to 10 and place an equal sign beside each number.
3. Challenge students to find all of the addition combinations for each value and write the expressions on their charts in the rows beside the numbers. Complete one box together: $6 = 0 + 6$, $1 + 5$, $2 + 4$, $3 + 3$, $4 + 2$, $5 + 1$, and $6 + 0$. Model how to read and write addition equations and discuss the commutative property of addition.
4. Allow students to work independently or with partners to complete the exercise for the remaining numbers. Students will likely need extra time to complete this activity, so you may continue the lesson during your next small-group lesson.

Name_____

## Add the cubes to solve each problem.

  makes _____ cubes.

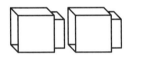    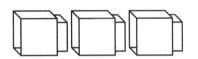  makes _____ cubes.

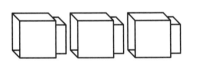    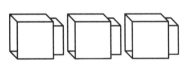  makes _____ cubes.

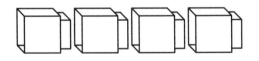  makes _____ cubes.

makes _____ cubes.

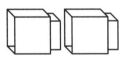  makes _____ cubes.

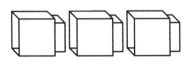    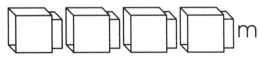  makes _____ cubes.

## Show another way to make 7 cubes.

Name_____

Draw and add to find how many. Write the number sentence.

_____ + _____ = _____

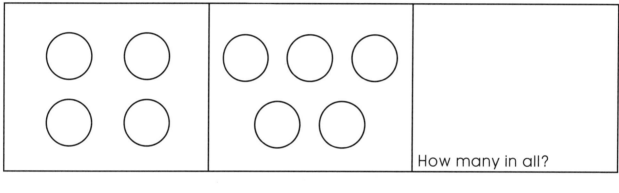

_____ + _____ = _____

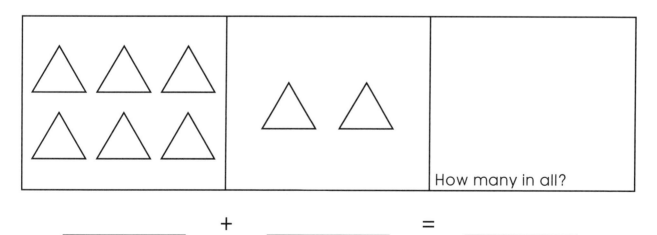

_____ + _____ = _____

Write or draw at least 2 different ways to make 10.

CD-104541 © Carson-Dellosa

Name_____

Solve each problem. Draw pictures to show your work. Then, write the related addition number sentence.

1 + 2 = _____

_____ + _____ = _____

4 + 1 = _____

_____ + _____ = _____

3 + 6 = _____

_____ + _____ = _____

5 + 5 = _____

_____ + _____ = _____

2 + 7 = _____

_____ + _____ = _____

6 + 4 = _____

_____ + _____ = _____

8 + 0 = _____

_____ + _____ = _____

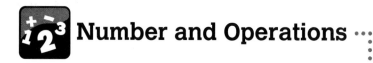

# Number and Operations

## Materials:
- Set of any 6 similar objects (for example, artificial flowers, large markers, or books)
- Counting chips
- Paper cups
- Flash cards (subtracting from 18 or less)
- Math journals
- Linking cubes
- Activity sheets (pages 23–25)

## Mini-Lesson

1. Invite 2 students to come to the front of the room. Give one student 6 similar objects, such as books, and the other student nothing.
2. Tell a story as the volunteers act it out. Say, "Kevin has 6 books. Tasha has 0 books. Kevin is such a great friend that he is going to give Tasha 1 book. How many books does Kevin have left?"
3. Continue by having the first student give the other student 1 to 2 objects at a time until he has none left. Then, say, "How many books does Kevin have left? How many books does Tasha have now? The teacher comes and takes away 4 books from Tasha. How many does she have left?"
4. As you tell the story, emphasize the phrases *give away*, *take away*, and *have left*.
5. End by saying, "Tasha has 2 books left. What do you think Tasha should do?" (Give 1 book to Kevin.)

## Group 1 ◯

### Decomposing Sets
1. Give each student 1 paper cup and 8 counting chips.
2. Instruct students to place their chips on the table in front of them. Explain that when you say *cup*, they should place 1 chip in their cups and count how many chips are left.
3. After each time you say cup, ask questions to spur discussion. For example, "How many chips did you have before I said cup? How many do you have left? Do you have less/fewer or more than you had before?"
3. Once students have no chips left, start again. This time, explain that when you say cup, students should place 2 chips in their cups. Again, ask questions after each step of the process.
4. Repeat by having students subtract 1 to 4 chips at a time.

## Group 2 ◻

### Subtracting from 10
1. Give each student 1 paper cup and 10 counting chips.
2. Instruct students to place their chips on the table in front of them. Explain that they will place the chips that are taken away in their cups.
3. Ask, "How many chips do you have? If you take 2 chips away, how many do you have left?" Remind students to place 2 chips in their cups. Continue subtracting 1 to 3 chips at a time.
4. Introduce how to use and read a minus sign by writing an equation for each story problem. Have students record the equations in their math journals as you write them on the board.
5. Repeat steps 3 and 4 by taking away 4 to 10 chips at a time.

## Group 3 △

### Subtraction Facts
1. Model how to read a subtraction equation and find the answer using counting chips. For example, "6 minus 4 equals what? If I have 6 chips, and I take away 4 chips, how many do I have left? I have 2 chips left."
2. Give each student 10 subtraction flash cards and 18 counting chips.
3. Tell students to use the counting chips to help them solve their sets of subtraction equations.
4. Have students record the problems and the answers in their math journals as they work.
5. If time allows, have students exchange sets of flash cards and repeat the activity with new problems.

Name_____

# Use linking cubes to help you solve the problems. How many cubes are left?

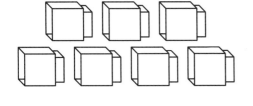 Take away 6 leaves _____ cube.

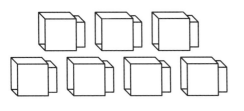 Take away 2 leaves _____ cubes.

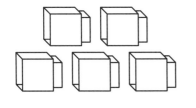 Take away 3 leaves _____ cubes.

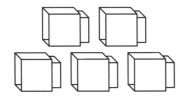 Take away I leaves _____ cubes.

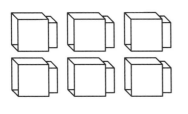 Take away 5 leaves _____ cube.

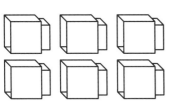 Take away 4 leaves _____ cubes.

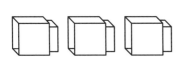 Take away 3 leaves _____ cubes.

Name_____

Solve the problems. Draw an X on each apple that you give away.

10 apples – 2 apples = _____ apples

10 apples – 1 apple = _____ apples

10 apples – 3 apples = _____ apples

10 apples – 6 apples = _____ apples

10 apples – 4 apples = _____ apples

**24**

Name_____

## Solve the problems. Draw pictures to show your work.

$4 - 2 =$ _____

$6 - 3 =$ _____

$9 - 1 =$ _____

$5 - 5 =$ _____

$10 - 4 =$ _____

$3 - 0 =$ _____

Ebony had 7 apples. She gave 2 away. How many apples does she have left? _____ apples

Write the number sentence: _____ − _____ = _____

Felipe had 5 apples. He gave some away. He has 2 apples left. How many did he give away? _____ apples

Write the number sentence: _____ − _____ = _____

# Number and Operations

**Objective**
Skip count by 2s, 5s, and 10s.

**Materials:**
- Overhead projector
- Hundred chart transparency
- Student copies of hundred chart
- Transparent, colored chips
- Colored pencils
- Nickels and dimes
- Activity sheets (pages 27–29)

## Mini-Lesson

1. Display a hundred chart on the overhead projector.
2. Place chips on the even numbers 2 to 10. Explain, "If we skip count by 2s, we say every second number like this: 2, 4, 6, 8, 10." Have students count with you as you point to and say each number.
3. Ask, "How will I know what numbers to skip and what numbers to say if I want to count by 5s to 20?" Discuss and cover the 5s with chips. Have students count with you as you point.
4. Say, "Now, we are going to count by 10s to 50. What numbers will we use to count?" Discuss and cover the 10s with chips. Have students count with you as you point.
5. Count again by 2s to 10, 5s to 20, and 10s to 50. Each time, encourage students to notice patterns in the numbers on the chart.

## Group 1 ○

**Skip Counting to 50**
1. Give each student a hundred chart and 5 chips.
2. Model how to whisper odd numbers and say even numbers loudly from 1 to 10. For example, "one, TWO, three, FOUR, five, SIX . . ." As you say each even number, place a chip on that number. Have students copy what you did to skip count by 2s to 10 on their own charts.
3. Model the same process for skip counting by 5s to 20 and then have students skip count using their own charts and chips.
4. Count by 10s to 50 for the group as students place chips on the 10s. Ask, "What do those numbers have in common?" (The last digit is always 0.) Count by 10s together.
5. Have each student count by 2s, 5s, and 10s with or without their charts.

## Group 2 □

**Skip Counting Patterns**
1. Give each student a hundred chart and 3 different colored pencils.
2. As a group, use the chart as a reference to skip count verbally by 2s, 5s, and 10s to 100.
3. Have students lightly color their charts to show counting by 2s in one color, counting by 5s in another color, and counting by 10s in a third color.
4. Begin a discussion about patterns observed on each chart. Ask, "Do you see any patterns when we count by 2s? 5s? 10s?" "What numbers are in multiple sets?"

## Group 3 △

**Skip Counting to 100**
1. Give each student a hundred charts and 100 chips.
2. Check for understanding by asking each student to count by 2s, 5s, and 10s either with or without the chart.
3. Demonstrate how skip counting can help us count groups of things faster (the foundation of multiplication). Place 20 chips on the table. Model how to pair them and count by 2s.
4. Have students count groups of chips by 2s, 5s, and 10s to 100. Remind students to use their charts if they need help.
5. Further challenge students to count by 5s with tally marks or nickels and by 10s with dimes.

Name_____

Follow the directions to color the number charts.
Skip count by 2s. Color the boxes with those numbers yellow.

| 1 | 2 | 3 | 4 | 5 | 6 | 7 | 8 | 9 | 10 |
|---|---|---|---|---|---|---|---|---|----|

Skip count by 5s. Color the boxes with those numbers blue.

| 1 | 2 | 3 | 4 | 5 | 6 | 7 | 8 | 9 | 10 |
|----|----|----|----|----|----|----|----|----|----|
| 11 | 12 | 13 | 14 | 15 | 16 | 17 | 18 | 19 | 20 |

Skip count by 10s. Color the boxes with those numbers green.

| 1 | 2 | 3 | 4 | 5 | 6 | 7 | 8 | 9 | 10 |
|----|----|----|----|----|----|----|----|----|----|
| 11 | 12 | 13 | 14 | 15 | 16 | 17 | 18 | 19 | 20 |
| 21 | 22 | 23 | 24 | 25 | 26 | 27 | 28 | 29 | 30 |
| 31 | 32 | 33 | 34 | 35 | 36 | 37 | 38 | 39 | 40 |
| 41 | 42 | 43 | 44 | 45 | 46 | 47 | 48 | 49 | 50 |

Name_____

Follow the directions and write the numbers.

Skip count by 2s.

2, 4, 6, 8, ____, ____, ____, ____, ____, ____

Skip count by 5s.

5, 10, 15, ____, ____, ____, ____, ____, ____, ____

Skip count by 10s.

10, 20, 30, 40, ____, ____, ____, ____, ____, ____

Write numbers on the lines as you skip count by 2s to count the chips.

◯ ◯ ◯ ◯ ◯ ◯ ◯ ◯ ◯ ◯
◯ ◯ ◯ ◯ ◯ ◯ ◯ ◯ ◯ ◯

____ ____ ____ ____ ____ ____ ____ ____ ____ ____

Give this activity sheet to your teacher. Skip count aloud by 2s, 5s, and 10s. Ask your teacher to write how far you can skip count without any help.

I can skip count by 2s to _____ by myself.

I can skip count by 5s to _____ by myself.

I can skip count by 10s to _____ by myself.

**28**

Name_____

# Skip count to count the total number of shapes in each group. Write the numbers on the lines as you count.

Skip count by 2s to count the triangles.

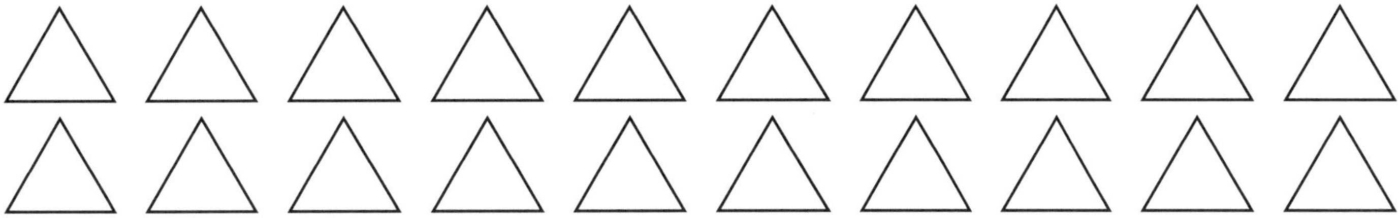

△ △ △ △ △ △ △ △ △ △

△ △ △ △ △ △ △ △ △ △

___ ___ ___ ___ ___ ___ ___ ___ ___ ___

Skip count by 5s to count the circles.

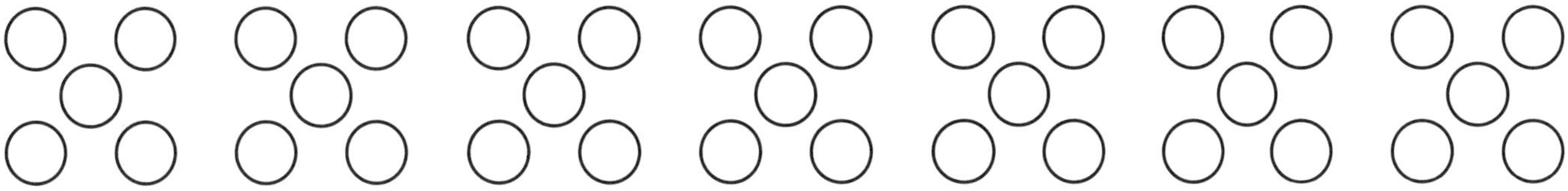

___ ___ ___ ___ ___ ___ ___ ___

Skip count by 10s to count the squares.

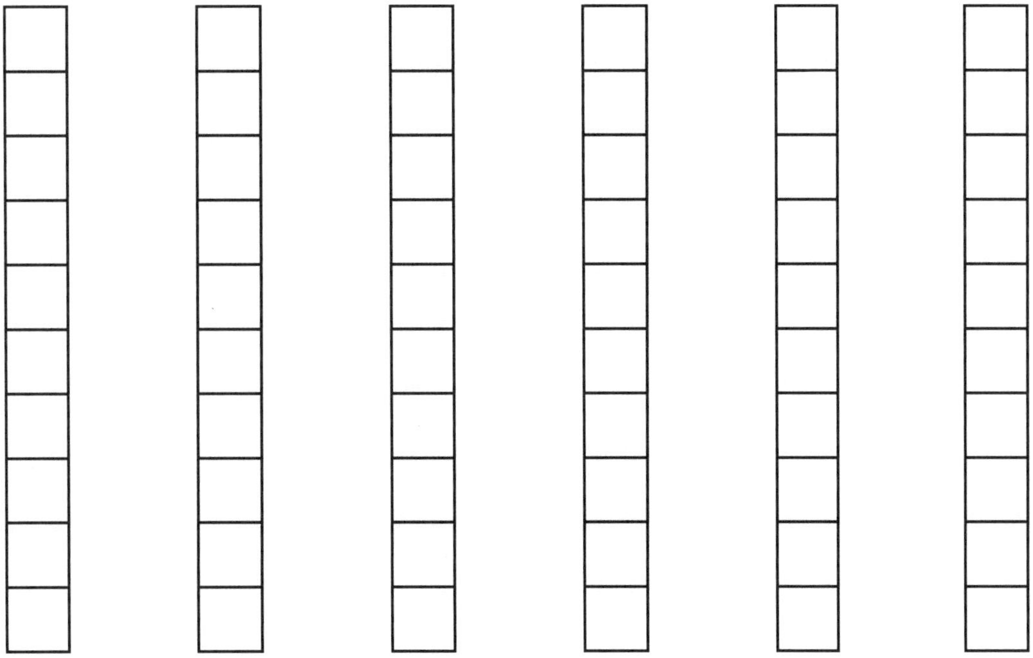

___ ___ ___ ___ ___ ___

# Number and Operations

**Materials:**
- Stickers
- *The Doorbell Rang* by Pat Hutchins (Greenwillow Books, 1994)
- Counting chips
- Math journals
- Activity sheets (pages 31–33)

**Objective**

Explore division by sharing equally.

## Mini-Lesson

1. Gather 12 lollipops. Invite 6 students to stand at the front of the room. Say, "I have 12 lollipops that I would like to share with all of you." Give each student 1 lollipop. Then, point out that you still have 6 lollipops left. Ask, "What should I do with these lollipops?" The class will likely recommend that you give each of the 6 students 1 more lollipop each. Do as they suggest.
2. Collect lollipops and invite a group of 12 new students to stand. Distribute lollipops to the new group, but give 3 to the 10th student and none to the 11th or 12th student. The class will likely point out your error. Collect lollipops and redistribute equally. Emphasize that you should share equally.
3. Repeat step 1 with 2, 3, and 4 students. (Note: Collect lollipops or share with the class.)

## Group 1 ◯

**Dividing into 2 Equal Groups**

1. Read *The Doorbell Rang* to the group. Encourage students to discuss each situation as you read.
2. Place 10 counting chips on the table. Tell students to imagine that the chips are cookies. Model the "one for me, one for you" strategy for sharing equally as you divide the chips (cookies) into 2 equal groups.
3. Give each student 2 chips. Have students divide 2 chips into 2 equal groups using the "one for me, one for you" strategy. Give 2 more chips to each student. Again, have students divide the chips into 2 equal groups. Repeat with 6, 8, and 10 chips.
4. Ask students to explain in their math journals what they know about sharing equally.

## Group 2 ▢

**Dividing into 2 and 3 Equal Groups**

1. Follow steps 1 to 3 from the Group 1 lesson with 2, 4, and 6 chips (cookies).
2. After dividing 6 chips into 2 groups of 3, ask students to find another way to share the "cookies" equally (3 groups of 2 or 6 groups of 1). Model how to modify the strategy to be "one for me, one for you, one for you."
3. Give each student 2 more chips. Encourage students to find more than one way to divide the chips. Repeat with 10 chips.
4. Challenge students to work together to discover at least 3 ways to divide 12 equally. As they discover each way, have students record their findings in their math journals and title the entries "How to Share 12 Equally."

## Group 3 △

**Dividing into 2, 3, and 4 Equal Groups**

1. Give students 10 chips each. Review how to divide 2, 4, 6, 8, and 10 chips equally into 2 groups. Ask, "Which number of chips can be divided equally into 3 groups? 4 groups?"
2. Give students 2 more chips (= 12). Encourage them to find as many ways as possible to divide the chips into equal groups.
3. Take away 3 chips (= 9). Ask, "Can 9 cookies be divided into 2 equal groups?" Have students explain why or why not. Ask, "Do you think 9 cookies can be divided into equal groups?" Tell students to make predictions and then prove them.
4. Give students 6 more chips (= 15) and repeat step 3. Explain that some numbers cannot be divided equally without something being left over.
5. Have students write in their math journals describing situations where they might have to share equally.

CD-104541  © Carson-Dellosa

Name_____

Use counting chips to divide each number into 2 equal groups. Draw circles to show your work.

2

| | |
|---|---|
| | |

4

| | |
|---|---|
| | |

6

| | |
|---|---|
| | |

8

| | |
|---|---|
| | |

10

| | |
|---|---|
| | |

Name_____

Draw a line to divide each set of shapes into 2 equal groups.

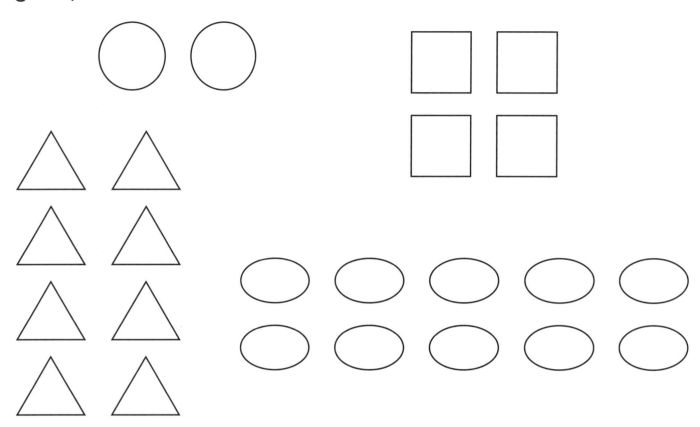

Divide 6 and 12 into equal groups. Draw circles to show your work.

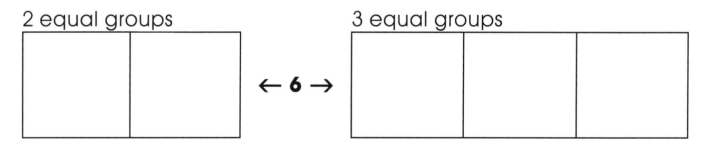

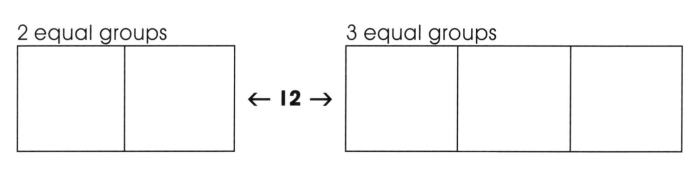

Name_____

Write *yes* or *no* in each box to show which numbers can be divided into equal groups. Use counting chips to help you. The first two have been done for you.

| Number | 2 equal groups | 3 equal groups | 4 equal groups |
|---|---|---|---|
| 5 | no | no | no |
| 6 | yes | yes | no |
| 7 | | | |
| 8 | | | |
| 9 | | | |
| 10 | | | |
| 11 | | | |
| 12 | | | |
| 13 | | | |
| 14 | | | |
| 15 | | | |

# Number and Operations

## Objective
Determine place value of ones and tens using base ten blocks.

**Materials:**
- Paper models of base ten blocks (10 units, 3 rods)
- Magnets or tape
- Base ten blocks (units and rods)
- Place value charts (H, T, O)
- 10-sided dice
- Activity sheets (pages 35–37)

## Mini-Lesson

1. Use magnets or tape to display the paper base ten blocks on the board. Line up 1 rod (left) next to 10 units (right). Point to each unit as students count aloud and point to each section of the rod as they count aloud. Encourage students to describe what they see (for example, same height, same number of units, or 1 rod = 10 units).
2. Explain, "You cannot have more than 9 in any place, so when you get 10, you *group* them together and *move* them over." (Dramatically point left to emphasize moving over.)
3. Clear the board. Place 1 unit at a time on the board as students count. After placing 10 units, remove them from the board and place 1 rod in the tens place. Repeat until you have 35.
4. As you model the process, use the terms *ones, units, tens, rods,* and *place value*.

## Group 1 ○

**Using Base Ten Blocks**
1. Give each student 10 units, 2 rods, and a place value chart.
2. Have students place base ten blocks on their charts as they count aloud together from 1 to 20. Model along with students. When you place 10 units in the ones place, dramatically emphasize grouping them together, trading 10 units in for 1 rod, and moving over to the tens place.
3. Using base ten blocks, show a value from 1 to 20. Ask students to show the same value on their charts using base ten blocks and then identify the number. Repeat several times.
4. Invite students to take turns being the "teacher" and model a number with base ten blocks for the group.

## Group 2 ▢

**Regrouping Ones**
1. Give each student 25 units, 2 rods, and a place value chart. Have students take turns modeling numbers from 1 to 25 using base ten blocks. Ask questions such as, "How many rods are in the tens place? How many units are in the ones place? How do you know the value is 21?"
2. Give students any number of unit cubes from 1 to 25. Ask, "Do you have more or less/fewer than 10 cubes? Can you place all of your cubes in the ones place? Why or why not?" Guide students to count out groups of 10 ones and replace them with rods.
3. Once students' models are complete, have them share their numbers and compare with the original count of unit cubes.
4. Repeat with various numbers of unit cubes.

## Group 3 △

**Modeling Numbers**
1. Give pairs of students 9 units, 9 rods, a place value chart, and 2 ten-sided dice.
2. Write 48 on the board. Have students use their blocks to show the number on their charts. Ask, "What number is in the ones place? What does the 4 mean?" Repeat with several numbers.
3. Have student pairs play this game: Players take turns rolling the dice and using their blocks to model the greatest number they can make with the 2 digits rolled. Players record each round of numbers and compare to see which player made the greatest number.
4. After 10 times, have students repeat the game, trying to make the lowest numbers.

Name_____

# Model each number with base ten blocks. Write the number.

| Tens | Ones |
|------|------|
| | □ |
| | □ □ □ |
| | □ □ □□ □□ □□ |
| ▯ | |
| ▯ | □ □ |

The number is _____.

The number is _____.

The number is _____.

The number is _____.

The number is _____.

Name_____

Circle groups of 10 units. Draw the value correctly using units and rods. Identify the number.

| Tens | Ones |
|------|------|
|      |      |

The number is _____.

| Tens | Ones |
|------|------|
|      |      |

The number is _____.

| Tens | Ones |
|------|------|
|      |      |

The number is _____.

Name_____

Use each pair of digits to make the greatest and the lowest numbers. Draw a picture for each number using units and rods.

Greatest Number

| Tens | Ones |
| --- | --- |
| | |

Lowest Number

| Tens | Ones |
| --- | --- |
| | |

8 and 4

Greatest Number

| Tens | Ones |
| --- | --- |
| | |

Lowest Number

| Tens | Ones |
| --- | --- |
| | |

2 and 5

Greatest Number

| Tens | Ones |
| --- | --- |
| | |

Lowest Number

| Tens | Ones |
| --- | --- |
| | |

6 and 7

 **Algebra**

## Objective

Sort and classify objects and determine what does not belong in a set.

**Materials:**
- Overhead projector
- Pattern blocks
- Math manipulatives
- Crayons, colored pencils, and markers
- Blank Venn diagrams
- Activity sheets (pages 39–41)

## Mini-Lesson

1. Before the lesson, gather 12 pattern blocks: 5 squares, 3 parallelograms, 3 trapezoids, and 1 triangle.
2. Place the shapes on the overhead projector and ask students to describe what they see (for example, 12 shapes or more squares than any other shape).
3. Say, "Let's sort these shapes. Let's put them into groups." Have students make suggestions for sorting or invite volunteers to sort the shapes on the overhead projector.
4. Students will likely sort the shapes by type. When that happens, have students explain why the shapes are sorted as such and then ask, "Which shape does not belong in this group? Why?" (The triangle, because it is the only shape that does not have 4 sides. Or, it is the only shape by itself.)

## Group 1 ○

### Determine What Does Not Belong

1. Gather a variety of math manipulatives (linking cubes, pattern blocks, counting bears, colored chips, etc.) in a variety of colors.
2. Instruct the group to close their eyes as you choose a set of 3 to 4 similar objects (same color or all bears, etc.) and 1 different item. Display the objects on the table and have students open their eyes.
3. Ask students to identify which object does not belong and why. Repeat as desired. Then, invite students to create their own sets for the group.
4. Have students work together to sort the objects by color and then by type. You may even use this activity as a fun way to organize the classroom.

## Group 2 □

### Sorting Rules

1. Give each student 20 math manipulatives (linking cubes, pattern blocks, counting bears, colored chips, etc.) in a variety of colors.
2. Have students sort the manipulatives as they choose.
3. Ask students to explain their "rules" for sorting (for example, by color, size, shape, or function).
4. Challenge students to sort the same manipulatives in a different way and explain what they did.
5. Give each student 1 more manipulative. Have each student justify whether the object belongs or does not belong in each of the groupings.
6. Invite students to try to add to each other's groupings by guessing the rules used.

## Group 3 △

### Using a Venn Diagram

1. Give each student crayons, colored pencils, and markers (8 to 12 of each).
2. Have students sort the art supplies into 2 groups: red in one group and markers in another.
3. Ask, "Which objects do not belong in either set? Do any objects belong in both sets?"
4. Draw 2 overlapping circles on paper. Label one circle red and the other circle marker. Place a red marker in the overlapping section, a red crayon and a red pencil in the red circle, and the remaining markers in the marker circle. Place objects that do not belong in either circle outside the diagram.
5. Give students 1 blank Venn diagram each and have them label each circle with a category and place the objects in the correct sections. Have students switch diagrams with partners and sort again.

Name_____

## Gather the number of pattern blocks as shown.

  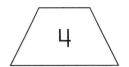 

## Sort the blocks. Draw pictures to show how you sorted them.

## Look at the pictures. Draw an X on the picture that does not belong in each set.

  |

  |

  |

  |

  |

  |

Name_____

Sort the shapes in 2 different ways. Draw pictures and describe how you sorted the shapes.

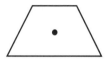  

Sort 1




How did you sort the shapes? _____

Sort 2




How did you sort the shapes? _____

Look at the shapes. Do they belong with any of your sorted sets? Why or why not?

 _____

 _____

Name_____

# Write the numbers 1 to 25 in the correct sections of the Venn diagram.

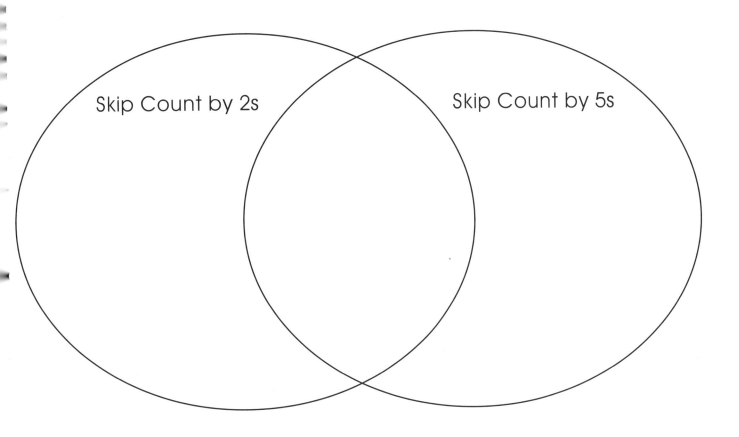

Skip Count by 2s      Skip Count by 5s

## Look at the numbers. Draw an X on the number that does not belong in each set.

| 11 | 6 | 7 | 5 | | 8 | 3 | 4 | 6 |
|----|---|---|---|---|---|---|---|---|
| 40 | 50 | 62 | 70 | | 1 | 20 | 15 | 5 |

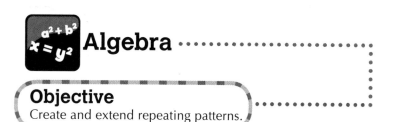

# Algebra

## Objective
Create and extend repeating patterns.

**Materials:**
- Linking cubes
- Pattern blocks
- Small whiteboards
- Write-on/wipe-away markers
- Math journals
- Activity sheets (pages 43–45)

## Mini-Lesson

1. Rhythmically say, "Be my echo." (Class: Be my echo.) "Repeat after me." (Class: Repeat after me.)
2. Clap a pattern such as clap-clapclap-clap pause. Wait for students to repeat. Do this several times with various pattern units. Get creative by adding foot stomps or lap taps to the pattern.
3. Begin a discussion by introducing the words *pattern*, *repeat*, and *extend*.
4. Have students stand in a circle. Explain that you are going to clap a pattern. Then, one by one, have each student (in order) join the pattern by clapping along. Keep the pattern simple (for example, clap-clap-clap-pause). Students will have fun with this repeating pattern as it makes its way around the room.

## Group 1 ◯

**Extending Patterns**
1. Before the lesson, create 1 linking cube pattern for each student in the group plus 1 extra. Be sure that each pattern is different in some way (AB, ABC, AAB, ABB, etc.).
2. Give 1 cube set to each student, keep 1 for yourself, and place extra, unattached cubes in the center of the table.
3. Use your cube set to model how to "read" and extend the pattern. Say, "I see 2 colors that repeat: red, blue, red, blue. I can use that pattern to determine what comes next: red, blue. I can also read it as this: AB AB AB."
4. Invite students to talk about their patterns and use the unattached cubes to extend the patterns by one unit. Switch sets and repeat.

## Group 2 ▢

**Translating Patterns**
1. Use pattern blocks to create a simple AB repeating pattern. Model how to "read" the pattern by color, shape, or pattern unit (for example, AB AB AB) as well as how to extend the pattern.
2. Have students create their own patterns using the blocks (for example, AB, ABC, AAB, ABB) and "read" their patterns by color, shape, or pattern unit.
3. Pair students with partners. In each pair, have one partner create a pattern with linking cubes and then challenge his partner to form the same pattern with pattern blocks. Have them switch roles and repeat.
4. Have students label a page in their math journals with a pattern name (for example, AAB) and then draw the pattern in at least 3 different ways (for example, colors, shapes, or objects.)

## Group 3 △

**Shape Patterns**
1. On a whiteboard, draw an ABC repeating pattern using shapes (for example, circle, square, triangle, circle, square, triangle).
2. Give each student a whiteboard and a write-on/wipe-away marker. Have students draw the patterns on their own whiteboards. Ask, "What is the repeated unit in this pattern? How do we read the pattern using letters? How can we extend this pattern?" Have students circle the repeated section, label the pattern with its letter name, and extend the pattern twice.
3. Repeat with more complex repeating patterns (for example, AABC, ABCB, ABBB, or ABBAC) and discuss each one together. Show students how the patterns cannot only be described by letters but also by numbers.

Name_____

# Use linking cubes to create each pattern. Color the cubes to show and extend the pattern.

red    blue    red    blue

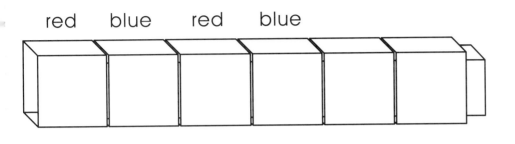

yellow  green  yellow  green

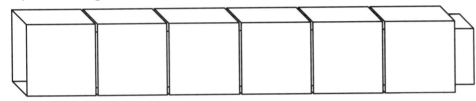

black  white  blue  black  white  blue

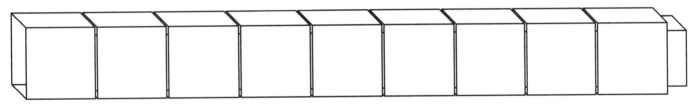

green  green  purple  green  green  purple

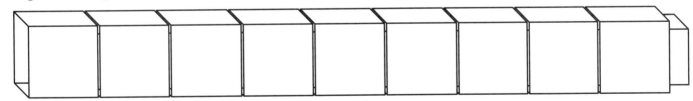

red  yellow  yellow  red  yellow  yellow

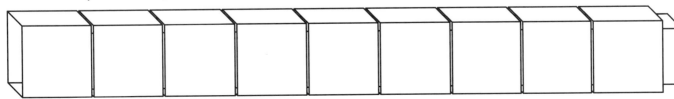

Name_____

Extend each pattern.

□ ○ △ □ ○ △ □ ○ △ ___ ___ ___ ___

○ □ □ ○ □ □ ___ ___ ___

Draw three different patterns to match each pattern name.

AB  _____

ABC  _____

AAB  _____

Copy each pattern using shapes.

44

Name_____

# Draw each pattern using shapes.

ABBA

ABCB

ABCD

 **Algebra**

**Materials:**
- Books
- Self-stick notes
- Blocks
- Small whiteboards
- Write-on/wipe-away markers
- Pattern blocks
- Several sets of number cards (1–5)
- Activity sheets (pages 47–49)

## Objective
Create and extend growing patterns.

## Mini-Lesson

1. Invite 3 volunteers to stand. Give the first student 2 books, the second student 4 books, and the third student 6 books.
2. Ask students to determine the pattern. Introduce the phrase *growing pattern*—a sequence that increases or decreases by the same amount. Have students explain why the book pattern is a growing pattern.
3. Invite 4 new volunteers to stand. Place 3 self-stick notes on the first student's shirt, 5 on the next, 2 on the next, and 4 on the next. Ask, "Is this a growing pattern?" Encourage students to explain their thinking. Ask, "Can we rearrange the students to show a growing pattern?"
4. Have volunteers arrange themselves in a growing pattern sequence (either increasing or decreasing). Have remaining students explain why this fits the definition of a growing pattern.

## Group 1 ◯

**Introducing Growing Patterns**
1. Take students to the block center.
2. Create a growing pattern with 4 to 5 blocks (for example, 1 block, 2 stacked blocks, 3 stacked blocks, etc.). Ask students to describe what they see. Explain that this is called a *growing pattern* because the pattern does not include a core repeating pattern unit, but the pattern increases in equal steps.
3. Invite each student to create 3 steps of a growing pattern with blocks. Have students switch seats and continue the growing patterns in front of them with 2 more steps. Encourage discussion as students create and extend the patterns. Repeat as desired.

## Group 2 ☐

**Growing Patterns**
1. Give each student 20 of the same pattern blocks and a set of number cards (1–5).
2. Model how to create a growing pattern by stacking the blocks and label each stack with a number card (for example, 1 triangle [1], 2 stacked triangles [2], and 3 stacked triangles [3]).
3. Have students build and label their own stacked block patterns and explain why they are growing patterns.
4. Write the numbers 1, 2, and 3 on a whiteboard. Challenge students to explain why it is a growing pattern. Write other growing patterns using 3 to 4 consecutive numbers up to 12 (for example, 7, 8, 9, 10) and some simple skip-counting patterns (for example, 2, 4, 6, 8). Discuss each pattern together.

## Group 3 △

**Increasing and Decreasing Number Patterns**
1. Write the numbers 5, 10, and 15 on a whiteboard. Have students explain why it is an increasing growing pattern. Write other growing patterns using 3 to 4 numbers.
2. Explore various counting patterns: counting by 1s, 2s, 5s, and 10s. Discuss the "rule" for each pattern and challenge students to determine what number would come next in each sequence.
3. Use the same counting patterns to write decreasing growing patterns.
4. Have students write their own increasing and decreasing growing number patterns. Invite each student to write one pattern on the whiteboard and have the group determine the rule.

Name_____

# Tell if each set of shapes shows a growing pattern. Circle *yes* or *no*.

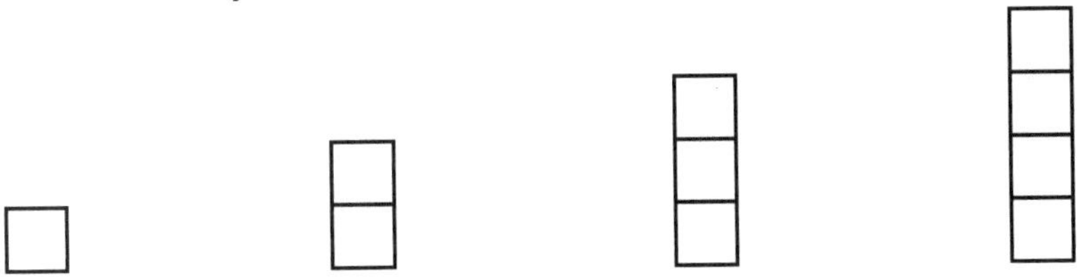

yes    no

yes    no

yes    no

yes    no

# Draw what comes next in each growing pattern.

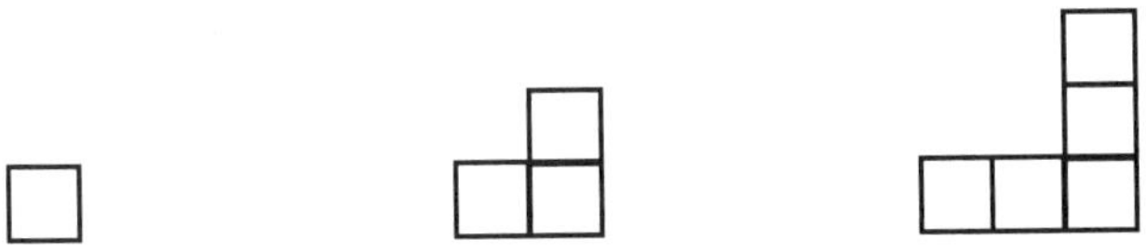

Name_____

Tell if each set of shapes shows a growing pattern.
Circle *yes* or *no*.

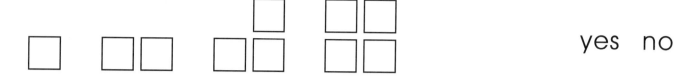

yes    no

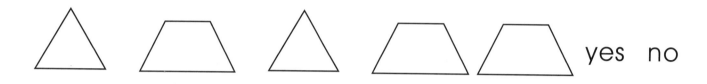

yes    no

Draw or write what comes next in each growing pattern.

2, 4, 6, _____

1, 3, 5, _____

7, 8, 9, _____

**48**

Name_____

# Draw or write the next two steps in each growing pattern.

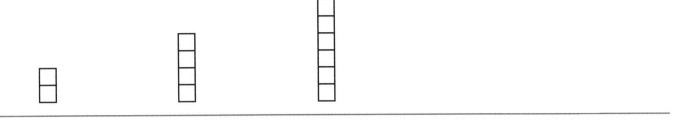

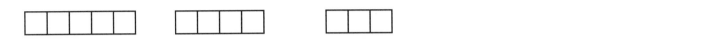

2, 3, 4, _____ , _____

12, 10, 8, _____ , _____

5, 10, 15, _____ , _____

40, 30, 20, _____ , _____

Draw or write an increasing growing pattern of your own.

Draw or write a decreasing growing pattern of your own.

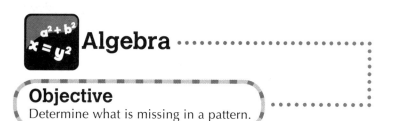 **Algebra**

## Objective
Determine what is missing in a pattern.

**Materials:**
- Pattern blocks
- Small whiteboards
- Write-on/wipe-away markers
- Counting chips
- Activity sheets (pages 51–53)

## Mini-Lesson

1. Play Who Is Missing? Ask a volunteer to stand in the hall for a few minutes. While that student is in the hall, select another student to hide somewhere in the classroom. After that student is hidden, have the remaining students change seats. Invite the student in the hall back and ask him to determine who is missing. Play as many times as you would like.
2. Explain that sometimes in math we need to determine what is missing.
3. Draw this pattern on the board: □ ○ □ ___ □ ○. Have students determine what shape is missing. Next, write this number sequence on the board: *1, 2, ___ , 4, 5, ___ , ___ , 8, ___ , 10.* Have students identify the missing numbers. Draw or write a few more examples on the board and discuss.

## Group 1 ○

**Missing Shapes**

1. Give each student pattern blocks, a small whiteboard, and a write-on/wipe-away marker.
2. Use pattern blocks to create a repeating pattern, but leave out 1 to 3 items (not in succession). Have students identify what items are missing. Then, have students choose blocks and correctly place them in the empty spaces.
3. Draw a repeating shape pattern on a whiteboard and leave blanks to show where shapes are missing. Have students draw the missing shapes on their whiteboards. Repeat several times.
4. Allow students to draw their own patterns with missing items on their whiteboards. Have them trade with partners and fill in the missing shapes.

## Group 2 □

**Missing Letters and Numbers**

1. Give each student a small whiteboard and a write-on/wipe away marker.
2. Write a consecutive letter sequence in alphabetical order on a whiteboard. Leave blanks to show where letters are missing. Have students write the missing letters on their whiteboards.
3. Repeat the process described in step 2, using consecutive number sequences counting by 1s, 2s and 5s. Ask, "How can you tell what numbers are missing?"
4. Invite students to write their own missing letter or number sequences. Have students exchange their whiteboards to solve each other's problems.

## Group 3 △

**Pattern Rules**

1. Give each student a small whiteboard and a write-on/wipe-away marker.
2. Write a number sequence counting by tens on a whiteboard and leave blanks to show where numbers are missing. Ask, "How can you tell what numbers are missing? What operation should you use to find the next number?"
3. Write a number sequence that decreases by 2s. Leave some of the spaces blank. Ask, "Now, what operation should you use to find the missing numbers?"
4. Explain to students that the operation they use plus the number they add or subtract is the pattern's rule.

Name_____

# Draw or write what is missing from each sequence.

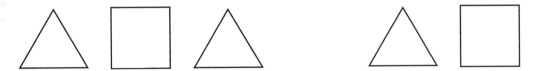

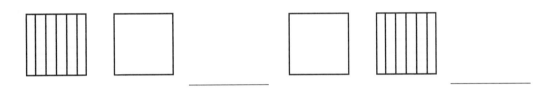

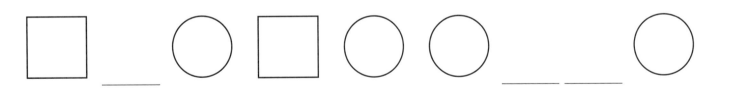

Name_____

# Write what is missing from each sequence.

A, _____ , C, D, _____ , F, G

_____ , K, L, M, _____ , O, _____

S, T, _____ , _____ , W, _____ , _____ , Z

_____ , Y, X, _____ , V, _____ , T

3, _____ , 5, _____ , 7, 8

_____ , 6, 7, _____ , 9, _____

2, 4, _____ , 8, _____ , 12

15, _____ , _____ , 12, 11, _____

Name_____

# Write what is missing from each sequence.

7, _____, 9, _____, _____, 12

2, _____, _____, 8, 10, _____, _____, 16

25, 20, _____, 10, _____, 0

# Write the rule for each pattern.

1, 3, 5, 7, 9, 11, 13, 15

Rule: _____

26, 28, 30, 32, 34, 36, 38

Rule: _____

100, 90, 80, 70, 60, 50, 60, 50, 40

Rule: _____

# Measurement

## Objective

Compare and describe objects based on length and weight.

**Materials:**
- Unsharpened pencils, envelopes, small books
- Small and large paper clips
- Pan balance
- Math journals
- Activity sheets (pages 55–57)

## Mini-Lesson

1. Ask students to select 1 object each from the classroom and bring the objects to their desks or the classroom's whole-group meeting space.
2. Write the words *length, shorter,* and *longer* on the board.
3. Select 1 student to stand and show an object. Ask, "Who has something *shorter* than this (object)?" Compare the 2 objects and have the newest volunteer explain why her object is shorter.
4. Instruct the first student to sit and the second to remain standing. Ask, "Who has something *longer* than this (object)?" Compare the 2 objects and have the newest volunteer explain why his object is longer.
5. Repeat this process several times to reinforce the concepts of shorter and longer.
6. Follow the same steps to introduce the concepts of *weight, lighter,* and *heavier.*

## Group 1 ◯

### Describing Weight and Length

1. Gather short, long, light, and heavy objects to compare (for example, pencils, envelopes, small but heavy rocks, long but light paperback books, short but heavy hardcover chapter books, etc.)
2. Select 2 objects and place them on the table. Model how to describe their length and weight using comparative words. For example, "The paperback book is longer than the hardcover book, but the hardcover book is heavier."
3. Allow each student the opportunity to do the same. Encourage use of the words *length, shorter, longer, weight, lighter,* and *heavier.*
4. Ask, "Will the shorter object always be lighter? Will the longer object always be heavier?" Have students experiment with the objects and write their thoughts in their math journals.

## Group 2 ▢

### Compare and Order Objects

1. Gather short, long, light, and heavy objects to compare (see examples in the Group 1 lesson).
2. Have each student place any 3 objects in order from lightest to heaviest and then talk about the objects' weight using comparative words. Repeat the process, this time placing those same objects in order from shortest to longest. Discuss the object's length using comparative words.
3. Give each student a pencil, an envelope, a small book, a handful of small paper clips, and a pan balance. Model how to measure the length and the weight of each object in nonstandard units (paper clips).
4. Have students record their measurements in their math journals and order the objects from heaviest to lightest and from longest to shortest based on the objects' measurements.

## Group 3 △

### Measuring with Nonstandard Units

1. Gather objects to compare (see examples in the Group 1 lesson).
2. Without measuring, have students order the objects from lightest to heaviest and then talk about the objects' weight using comparative words. Repeat by having them order the objects from shortest to longest.
3. Place bowls of small and large paper clips and a pan balance on the table. Have students find the length of each object in nonstandard units, first using small paper clips and then using large paper clips. Have them record their results (for example, pencil = 12 small paper clips. Have students repeat with weight using the pan balance.
4. Have students share their results. Ask, "How did the measurements change when using different-sized paper clips? Why do you think the measurements changed?"
5. Have students write math journal entries about the reliability and the usefulness of nonstandard measuring.

Name_____

Circle the object in each pair that is lighter.

Circle the object in each pair that is heavier.

Circle the object in each pair that is shorter.

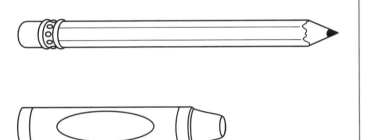
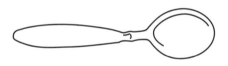
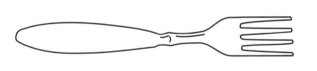

Circle the object in each pair that is longer.

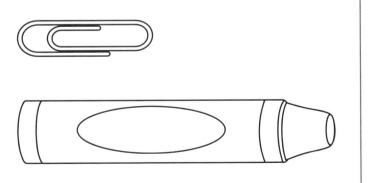

Name_____

Number each set of objects in order from 1 (lightest) to 3 (heaviest).

_____    _____    _____

_____    _____    _____

Measure the length of each box with small paper clips.

A  _____

B  _____

C  _____

Which box is the shortest—A, B, or C? _____

Which box is the longest—A, B, or C? _____

Name_____

Number the objects in order from 1 (lightest) to 4 (heaviest).

_____     _____     _____ 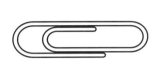    _____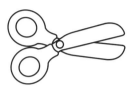

Measure the length of each box with small and large paper clips.

A

About ____ small paper clips long    About ____ large paper clips long

B

About ____ small paper clips long    About ____ large paper clips long

C

About ____ small paper clips long    About ____ large paper clips long

Which box is the shortest—A, B, or C? _____

Which box is the longest—A, B, or C? _____

How many paper clips does your pencil weigh?

About _____ small paper clips

About _____ large paper clips

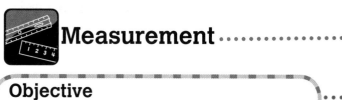

# Measurement

## Objective
Compare and describe containers based on capacity.

**Materials:**
- 10 containers of various heights
- Pitchers of dried beans
- Example of a cup, a pint, a quart, and a gallon
- Old magazines
- Activity sheets (pages 59–61)

## Mini-Lesson

1. Place 2 containers on the table.
2. Introduce the words volume and capacity (how much a container can hold). Ask students to predict which container has the greater volume or holds more.
3. Pour dried beans into what the class predicts is the container with the greater volume. Now, pour the beans into the other container. If beans still remain in the first container, then the students' prediction was correct. Repeat the process with two more sets of 2 containers.
4. Ask students to predict which of the 6 containers holds the most and which holds the least. Use the beans to test their predictions.

## Group 1 ◯

### Comparing Containers
1. Give each student 2 containers with different volumes and 1 pitcher of dried beans.
2. Ask students to predict which of their 2 containers has the greatest volume or holds more.
3. Have students fill the containers with beans to test their predictions as modeled in the mini-lesson.
4. Allow students time to compare containers. Encourage students to use words and phrases such as *holds more*, *holds less*, *holds about the same*, *volume*, and *capacity* as they work.
5. Ask, "Do taller containers always hold more than shorter containers? Why or why not?"

## Group 2

### Ordering Containers
1. Give each student 3 containers with different volumes and 1 pitcher of dried beans.
2. Before measuring, challenge students to arrange their containers in order from least to greatest volume (holds the least to holds the most).
3. Have students fill the containers with beans to test their predictions as modeled in the mini-lesson.
4. For those students who discovered that their predictions were wrong, provide support as they reorder their containers from least to greatest volume.
5. Ask, "Will the shortest container always hold the least? Why or why not?" Challenge students to find 2 containers that hold about the same amount but have different shapes.

## Group 3 △

### Cups, Pints, Quarts, and Gallons
1. Display a cup, a pint, a quart, and a gallon. Have students share what they know about the containers (for example, we use a cup when we bake, and we buy gallons of milk).
2. Give each student a plastic container. Ask, "Do you think your container holds about a cup, a pint, a quart, or a gallon?" Have students devise a plan for how to test their predictions using only the dried beans. Allow students time to experiment and then share their results as a group.
3. Put away all containers except for the cup and the gallon. Ask questions that require students to determine if they would use cups or gallons in various situations. For example, "Would we measure the amount of water in a bathtub in cups or gallons?"

Name_____

Circle the container in each set that holds more.

Circle the container in each set that holds less.

Find 2 containers above that hold about the same amount and color them blue.

Name_____

Number the containers in each set from 1 (holds the least) to 3 (holds the most).

_____        _____        _____

_____        _____        _____

Find 2 containers above that hold about the same amount and color them blue.

Name_____

Number the containers in each set from 1 (holds the least) to 4 (holds the most).

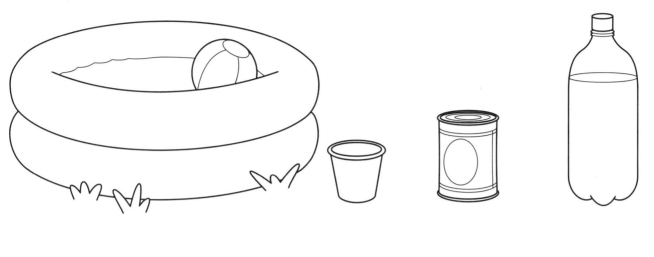

_____     _____     _____     _____

Which container above holds about the same amount as a drinking glass? Color the container blue.

Circle the best measurement for the amount each container holds.

cup     quart

pint     gallon

cup     quart

pint     gallon

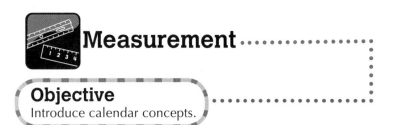

# Measurement

## Objective
Introduce calendar concepts.

**Materials:**
- Large classroom calendar
- Blank calendars
- Days of the Week cards (several sets)
- Months of the Year cards (several sets)
- Activity sheets (pages 63–65)

## Mini-Lesson

1. Use the classroom calendar to formally introduce calendar concepts. Begin by telling students that every calendar tells us what month it is. Have the class work together to name the months of the year. Write the months in a single column on the board off to the side.
2. Say, "We can also use the calendar to see what day it is." Have students name the days of the week and write them in a row across the top of the board (as seen on a calendar).
3. Explain that calendars also tell us what the date is. Define date as the number of the day. Point to each date on the classroom calendar as the class counts aloud.
4. Distribute the blank calendars. Walk students through the steps of creating their own calendars using months, days, and dates.

## Group 1 ○

### Basic Calendar Concepts
1. Ask students to bring their calendars from the mini-lesson to the math group.
2. Have students find the month on their calendars and then point to the days of the week as you say them together. Repeat the days of the week several times for reinforcement.
3. Next, have students point to each date as you count together. Say, "Find today's date."
4. Talk about the seasons of the year. Ask, "What season is it in July? October? What season is it at the beginning of the year? What season comes after summer?"

## Group 2 □

### Days of the Week
1. Using their calendars from the mini-lesson, invite students to share what they know about reading a calendar. Reinforce concepts as needed.
2. Talk about today's day and date. Ask questions such as, "What day will it be tomorrow?" and "What date was it yesterday?"
3. Have students point to the days of the week on their calendars as you say them together.
4. Give each student a set of Days of the Week cards. Have students shuffle the cards and then put them in order. Repeat as desired. Ask questions to reinforce day order. For example, "What day comes after Tuesday? What day comes between Thursday and Saturday?"

## Group 3 △

### Sequence of Days and Months
1. Discuss students' calendars. Talk about today's day and date. Ask questions such as, "What day was it on the 15th? How many days in (month) will you go to school? What is tomorrow's date? How many more days are there until Friday?"
2. Give each student a set of Days of the Week cards and Months of the Year cards. Instruct students to shuffle the 2 decks together, mixing the days and the months. Challenge the group to sort and order the cards appropriately.
3. After students have sequenced all of the cards, ask questions to reinforce month order and concepts of time within the year. Ask, "Which month comes before March? What are the summer months? In what months are your birthdays?"

Name_____

Number the seasons from 1 to 4 to put them in order.
The first one has been done for you.

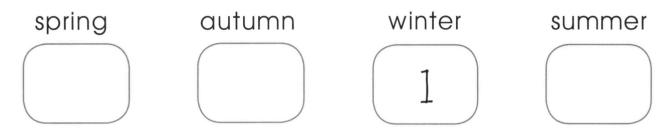

| spring | autumn | winter | summer |
|--------|--------|--------|--------|
|        |        | 1      |        |

Look at the calendar to answer the questions.

## May

| Sunday | Monday | Tuesday | Wednesday | Thursday | Friday | Saturday |
|--------|--------|---------|-----------|----------|--------|----------|
|        |        |         | 1         | 2        | 3      | 4        |
| 5      | ⑥      | 7 📖 Library | 8     | 9        | 10     | 11       |
| 12     | 13     | 14      | 15        | 16       | 17     | 18       |
| 19     | 20     | 21      | 22        | 23       | 24     | 25       |
| 26     | 27     | 28      | 29        | 30       | 31     |          |

What month is it? _____

How many days are in this month? _____

Today's date is circled. What day is it?_____

How many Thursdays are in this month?_____

On what day is library class? _____

Name_____

Number the days of the week from 1 to 7 to put them in order. The first one has been done for you.

Saturday  Monday  Thursday  Tuesday  Wednesday  Friday  Sunday

◯  ◯  ◯  ◯  ◯  ◯  ⬭1⬭

Look at the calendar to answer the questions.

## April

| Sunday | Monday | Tuesday | Wednesday | Thursday | Friday | Saturday |
|--------|--------|---------|-----------|----------|--------|----------|
|        | 1      | 2       | 3         | 4        | 5      | 6        |
| 7      | 8      | 9       | 10        | 11       | 12     | 13       |
| 14     | 15     | 16      | 17        | 18       | 19     | 20       |
| 21     | 22     | 23      | 24        | 25       | 26     | 27       |
| 28     | 29     | 30      |           |          |        |          |

What month is it? _____

How many days are in this month? _____

How many Tuesdays are in this month? _____

Today is the 11th. What day is it?_____

What day will it be tomorrow?_____

What was yesterday's date? _____

On what day and date is it someone's birthday?

day _____  date _____

**64**

Name_____

# Number the days of the week from 1 to 7.

| Saturday | Monday | Thursday | Tuesday | Wednesday | Friday | Sunday |
|---|---|---|---|---|---|---|
| ◯ | ◯ | ◯ | ◯ | ◯ | ◯ | ◯ |

# Number the months of the year from 1 to 12.

| April | January | September | November | June | March |
|---|---|---|---|---|---|
| ◯ | ◯ | ◯ | ◯ | ◯ | ◯ |

| October | December | May | February | August | July |
|---|---|---|---|---|---|
| ◯ | ◯ | ◯ | ◯ | ◯ | ◯ |

# Use the calendar to answer the questions.

## **February**

| Sunday | Monday | Tuesday | Wednesday | Thursday | Friday | Saturday |
|---|---|---|---|---|---|---|
| | 1 | 2 | 3 | 4 | 5 | 6 |
| 7 | 8 | 9 | 10 | 11 | 12 | 13 |
| 14 ♡ | 15 | 16 | 17 | 18 | 19 | 20 |
| 21 | 22 | 23 | 24 | 25 🎂 | 26 | 27 |
| 28 | | | | | | |

What month is it? _____

How many days are in this month? _____

On what day and date is Valentine's Day?

day _____     date _____

Tomorrow is library class. What is today's date? _____

If today is the eighth, what day will it be in 4 days? _____

What month comes before this month?_____

# Measurement

**Materials:**
- Analog and digital clock models
- Index cards
- Old magazines
- Practice analog clocks
- Construction paper
- Scissors
- Glue
- Crayons
- Activity sheets (pages 67–69)

## Mini-Lesson

1. Have students place their heads on their desks for 1 minute. Tell students to sit up when they think a minute has passed. Talk about what they could do in 1 minute.
2. Display an analog and a digital clock. Have students share what they know about time and clocks.
3. Write *second* near the bottom of the board (small but large enough to see). Explain, "A second is the smallest unit of time." Write *minute* above *second* (just a bit larger) and say, "Sixty seconds are in 1 minute." Watch as the second hand moves once around the analog clock.
4. Write *hour, day, week, month,* and *year* on the board in the same way (each word above and larger than the previous). Talk about the units of time and how they are connected.

## Group 1 ○

**Minutes vs. Hours**
1. Before the lesson, make T-charts on construction paper (one per student) and label the columns *minute* and *hour.*
2. Watch a minute pass on the classroom clock together. Explain that 60 seconds are in 1 minute, and 60 minutes are in 1 hour. Brainstorm some activities that take minutes and some that take hours (for example, brushing your teeth takes minutes, and going to school takes hours).
3. Give students the T-charts and the old magazines. Have students find pictures of activities that take minutes and hours, cut them out, and glue them in the appropriate places on their charts.
4. Allow students to share their charts and discuss why it might be important to keep track of time in the situations shown in their pictures.

## Group 2 □

**Parts of the Day**
1. Before the lesson, write *morning, afternoon, evening,* and *night* on index cards (3 to 5 cards of each word).
2. Begin a discussion about morning, afternoon, evening, and night. Talk about what activities happen during those times (for example, morning–eat breakfast, afternoon–play, night–go to bed).
3. Shuffle the cards and randomly place them facedown on the table. Invite students to take turns drawing a card, reading the word on the card, and identifying something they do during that time of day. Once students have drawn all of the cards, shuffle and repeat as desired.
4. Then, give each student a practice analog clock. Repeat the activity, this time having students show times on their clocks that match the times on the cards.

## Group 3 △

**Making Schedules**
1. Engage students in a discussion about schedules. Ask, "Why do people make schedules? Do your families have schedules?" Lead into, "What is *your* schedule? What do you do every day? Around what time do you _____?" Introduce and reinforce A.M. and P.M. while discussing.
2. Give each student a large sheet of construction paper.
3. Have students draw pictures to represent their daily schedules. For example, one student might draw a bowl of cereal, a school bus, some children learning, a soccer ball, a dinner table, a toothbrush, and the moon. Help students label their pictures with approximate times (for example, 2:00 P.M.).
4. Have students show the times on practice analog clocks as they share their schedules.

Name_____

Use yellow to color the activities that take minutes. Use blue to color the activities that take hours.

Draw a picture of an activity that takes about 1 minute and an activity that takes about 1 hour.

| about 1 minute | about 1 hour |
| --- | --- |
|  |  |

Name_____

Color the activities to show the time of day they would happen.

morning = yellow    evening = green

afternoon = red    night = blue

Draw pictures of activities that you do in the morning, the afternoon, and the evening. Draw hands on each clock to show a time that matches each activity.

| morning | afternoon | evening |
|---------|-----------|---------|
|         |           |         |

**68**

Name_____

# Number the activities in order from 1 to 8 to make a schedule for the day.

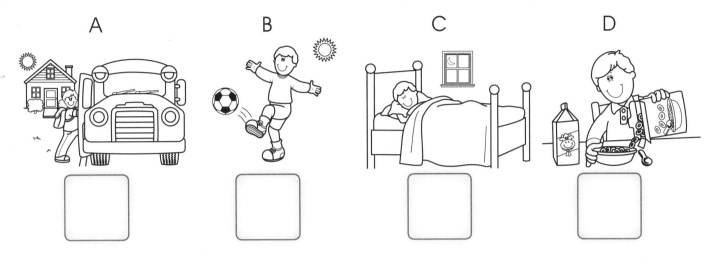

A  B  C  D

E  F  G  H

# Write the letter of each activity above that takes place at each time given. Look carefully to see if each time says A.M. or P.M.

6:00 P.M. _____          7:00 A.M. _____

7:30 A.M. _____          8:00 P.M. _____

4:00 P.M. _____          7:30 P.M. _____

10:00 A.M. _____          8:00 A.M. _____

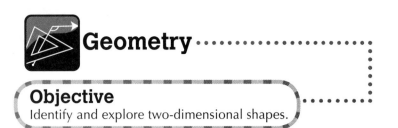

# Geometry

## Objective
Identify and explore two-dimensional shapes.

**Materials:**
- Paper shapes (1 per student)
- Index cards
- Small whiteboards
- Math journals
- Write-on/wipe-away markers
- Pattern blocks
- Activity sheets (pages 71–73)

## Mini-Lesson

1. Before the lesson, "hide" paper circles, triangles, squares, and rectangles of various colors around the classroom. Be sure the shapes are visible from students' seats.
2. Play I Spy by having students look for shapes of specific colors. Begin the game by saying, for example, "I spy a blue circle." Have the student who sees the shape first collect the shape and "spy" the next shape.
3. Once students find all of the shapes, tell students who have circles to stand in 1 corner of the room, students with triangles in another, and so on.
4. Ask each group to share observations about their shapes.
5. Send students around the classroom to search for real-world items (or faces of 3-D shapes) that match their shapes.

## Group 1 ◯

### Matching Shapes
1. Before the lesson, draw circles, triangles, and squares on index cards (4 of each).
2. Give each student 1 card and set aside any extras. Have each student say the name of the shape she is holding while showing it to the group. Passing it to the right, the next student will say its name. Once the shape circles back to the first student, have students pass the cards to the right and repeat.
3. Collect, shuffle, and lay the cards facedown on the table in a 3 x 4 array. Have students take turns flipping over 2 cards. If the shapes match, they keep the pair. If the shapes do not match, they flip the cards back over. Have students continue to play until they match all of the cards.

## Group 2 ▢

### Guessing Shapes
1. Have students name two-dimensional shapes with which they are familiar. Draw and label each shape on the board and have students do the same in their math journals.
2. Give each student a small whiteboard and a write-on/wipe-away marker (or paper and pencil).
3. Explain and then model how to play the game: Say, "Draw a shape on your whiteboard, but do not let anyone see the shape. Describe the shape without saying its name. You could say, 'This shape has no sides,' or 'A wheel is this shape,' rather than 'I drew a circle.' After you give your clue, everyone will draw what he or she thinks your shape is. If no one guesses it correctly, you will give another clue."
4. Have students take turns being the shape artist.

## Group 3 △

### Polygons
1. Place pattern blocks on the table and ask students to bring their math journals.
2. Have students name as many shapes as they can. Draw and label each shape on the board and have students do the same in their math journals.
3. Introduce the word polygon (a shape with many sides). Ask, "Are circles polygons? Why or why not?" Together, identify the names of various polygons.
4. Challenge students to use pattern blocks to find multiple ways to create a triangle, a square, a rectangle, and other polygons. Have students record their discoveries in their math journals. Can they make a small and a large triangle? Can they make congruent (same size) squares using different blocks?

Name_____

Trace each shape. Draw each shape on your own.

Color each ◯ blue. Color each △ yellow.
Color each ▢ orange.

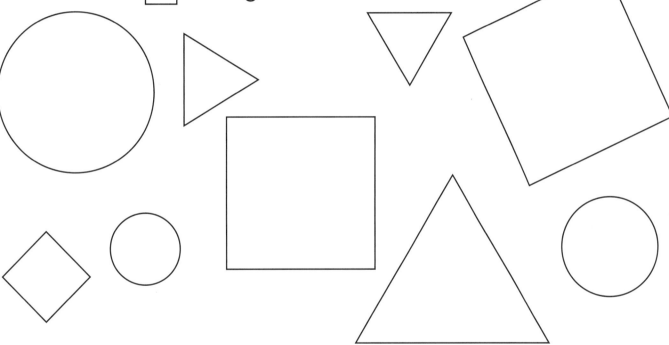

Draw a line from each shape word to the correct shape.

circle

triangle

square

Name_____

# Draw a line from each shape to the correct shape word.

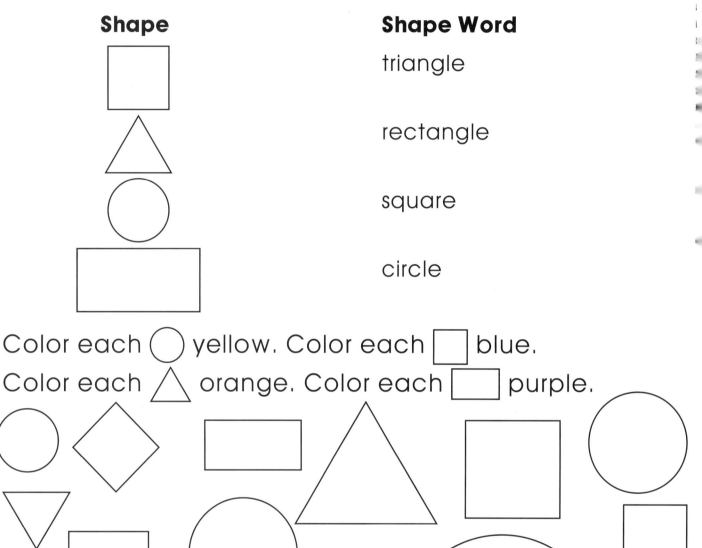

| **Shape** | **Shape Word** |
|---|---|
| | triangle |
| | rectangle |
| | square |
| | circle |

Color each ◯ yellow. Color each ☐ blue.
Color each △ orange. Color each ▭ purple.

Find I circle, I square, I triangle, and I rectangle in the classroom. On the back of this paper, draw or write what you found.

          CD-104541 © Carson-Dellosa

Name_____

# Draw a line from each shape to the correct shape word.

| **Shape** | **Shape Word** |
|---|---|

trapezoid

hexagon

parallelogram

rhombus

# Use pattern blocks to cover the hexagons. Trace and color the shapes to show what blocks you used.

I block

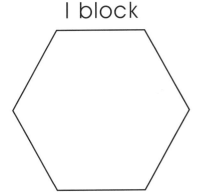

2 matching blocks

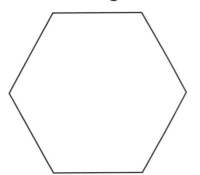

3 matching blocks

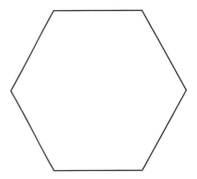

3 different blocks

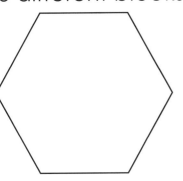

6 matching blocks

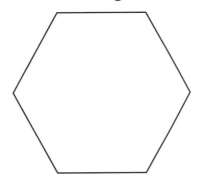

Can you find another way?

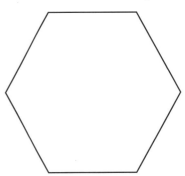

 **Geometry** ......................

## Objective

Sort and classify two-dimensional shapes based on number of sides.

## Mini-Lesson

1. Gather the number cards, a stack of 3 x 5 index cards, and a dark marker.
2. Ask students to name as many two-dimensional shapes as they can. Draw each shape neatly on an index card. If any shapes are missing, give hints or introduce the shapes to the class. Shapes should include circle, oval, different types of triangles, square, rectangle, rhombus, parallelogram, trapezoid, pentagon, hexagon, and octagon. (Note: Students do not need to know the names of all of the shapes for this lesson.)
3. Place the number cards across the tops of the pockets charts (3 on each chart).
4. Introduce the concept of "sides." As a group, sort shapes by the number of sides and place the shape cards under the correct numbers on the charts.

## Group 1 ○

### Counting Sides

1. Use the shape cards created during the mini-lesson. Distribute all of the cards and give each student a small whiteboard and a write-on/wipe-away marker.
2. Have students count the number of sides on each shape they have and, if they know it, name the shape. Provide support with identifying shapes as needed.
3. Ask students to draw their shapes on the whiteboards and number each side (for example, a square's sides would be numbered 1, 2, 3, and 4). Have students choose a new card and repeat.
4. Challenge the group to work together to sort the shapes by the number of sides. Then, have them sort the cards into the pocket charts.

## Group 2 □

### Drawing Shapes

1. Use the shape cards created during the mini-lesson. Shuffle the cards and place the deck facedown on the table.
2. Have students take turns flipping over the top card and counting the number of sides on each shape. Challenge students to name the shape, providing support as needed.
3. Give each student a small whiteboard and a write-on/wipe away marker (or paper and pencil).
4. Say a number (0, 3, 4, 5, 6, or 8) and have students draw a shape with that number of sides. As long as the shape drawn has the appropriate number of sides, the "answer" is correct. Remember that some shapes are irregular; however, if students draw common shapes, ask them to name the shapes.

## Group 3 △

### Different Shapes

1. Follow steps 1 and 2 from Group 2's lesson as a quick review.
2. Set aside all cards except for the square and the rectangle. Ask, "How are these shapes the same? How are they different?" Tell students that a square is a special kind of rectangle. Use a metaphor such as, "You are a girl, but your special name is Sarah."
3. Distribute small whiteboards and write-on/wipe-away markers (or paper and pencils).
4. Have students draw at least 4 different rectangles by varying length of sides.
5. Model how triangles look different as well. Draw a triangle with 3 equal sides (equilateral), a triangle with only 2 equal sides (for example, a tall isosceles triangle), and a triangle with no equal sides (scalene). Challenge students to draw at least 3 different triangles.

Name_____

# Count the sides on each shape. Write the number of sides inside each shape.

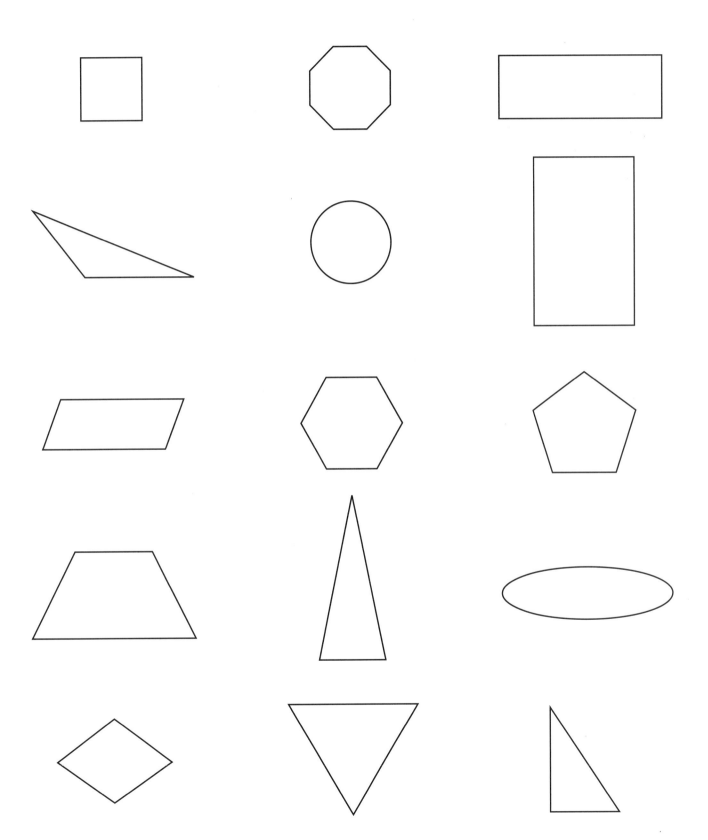

Name_____

Write a word from the word bank to answer each shape riddle.

| Word Bank | | | |
| --- | --- | --- | --- |
| circle | hexagon | octagon | oval |
| pentagon | rectangle | square | triangle |

I have 8 sides. People stop when they see me. What am I?

_____

I have 4 equal sides and 4 corners. What am I?

_____

I have 0 sides and look like an egg. What am I?

_____

I have 5 sides. Some people think I look like a house. What am I?

_____

I have 3 sides and 3 angles. What am I?

_____

I have 6 sides. I am not a stop sign.

_____

I have 0 sides. I am perfectly round. What am I?

_____

I have 2 sets of matching sides. What am I?

_____

    CD-104541 © Carson-Dellosa

Name_____

# Draw different shapes in the chart.

| Number of Sides | Shapes |
|---|---|
| 0 | |
| 3 | |
| 4 | |
| 5 | |
| 6 | |
| 8 | |

# Geometry

## Objective
Describe relative position of objects and follow directions.

**Materials:**
- Cardboard box
- Beanbags (2 different colors)
- Plastic cups
- Craft pom-poms
- Index cards
- Chart paper
- 3 x 3 charts
- Pencils
- Activity sheets (pages 79–81)

## Mini-Lesson

1. Place a box and 2 beanbags on the table. Invite 2 volunteers to stand near the table.
2. Give volunteers directions using positional words and phrases such as on, in, above, below, under, beside, next to, near, far away from, in front of, behind, between, and through. The directions could be what to do with their bodies (for example, "stand near the table" or "walk through the door"). Or, the directions could be what to do with the box and the beanbags (for example, "place a box between the beanbags and place the blue beanbag in the box").
3. Ask students to recall some of the positional words you used during the activity and write the words on the board.

## Group 1

### Following and Giving Directions
1. Give each student a plastic cup, 2 pom-poms, and an index card.
2. Direct students using positional words. For example, "Place 1 pom-pom next to the cup. Place the other pom-pom in the cup. Hold the index card above the cup. Place the index card on the cup. Hold 1 pom-pom in front of you. Now, move it behind you. Place the index card under you."
3. After practicing following directions with students, allow each student the opportunity to give directions to the rest of the group. You could even turn lesson this into a game of Simon Says.
4. End with a fun twist: Have students take turns using positional words to move you around the classroom.

## Group 2 □

### Positional Clues
1. Before the lesson, write each student's name on an index card and hide all of the cards throughout the classroom. Be sure to record specifically where you hid each card.
2. Ask students to summarize what they learned during the mini-lesson. Brainstorm positional words together and list them on chart paper.
3. Explain to students that you have hidden cards with their names somewhere in the classroom. Give students 1 direction at a time to help them find their cards. You might say, "Antonio, your card is under something. Evelyn, your card is next to something blue." Continue until all students find their cards.
4. Divide students into groups of 2 or 3, have them hide the name cards for each other, and give each other directions for finding them.

## Group 3 △

### Using Positional Words
1. Give each student a 3 x 3 chart. Discuss where left and right are on their charts. Have students mark their charts with an L and an R as a reference.
2. Give clues to where various numbers are placed on the chart. You might say, "The number 3 is in the center of the chart. The number 2 is below the number 3. The number 5 is in the top-right box. The number 1 is to the left of the number 5," and so on.
3. Once all of the spaces are filled, compare the placement of the numbers on the charts. Ask students to identify the relative position of each number. For example, "Where is the number 2?" (Below the number 3.)
4. If time allows, have students draw new 3 x 3 charts on the backs of their charts and repeat the activity by placing objects or pictures in the squares.

Name_____

# Where is the teddy bear? Write the number of the correct picture on each line.

1

2

3

4
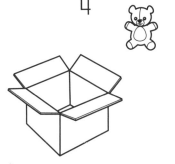

5
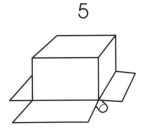

6

between _____

far _____

in _____

near _____

on _____

under _____

## Write the correct shape name to answer each question.

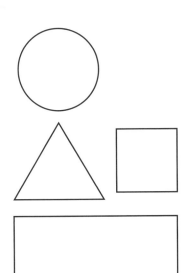

Which shape is **next to** the △?

_____

Which shape is **below** the △?

_____

Which shape is **above** the △?

_____

Name_____

Look at the picture and read the clues to solve the mystery.

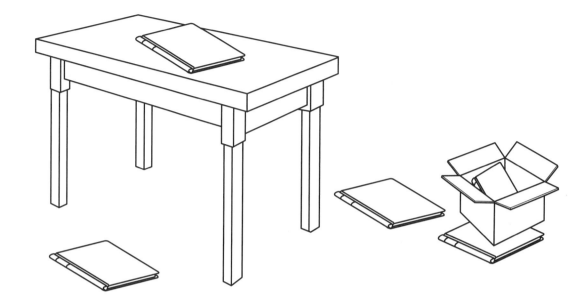

Write the clue numbers on the picture to show where each person placed the book.

Clues

1. Tara placed the book on something.

2. Ryan placed the book next to something.

3. Uma placed the book in something.

4. Sasha placed the book between two things.

   Where did Tyrone place the book? _____

Draw a pencil in two different places on the picture above. Use positional words to describe where you placed each pencil.

A. _____

B. _____

**80**

Name_____

# Follow the directions to complete the picture.

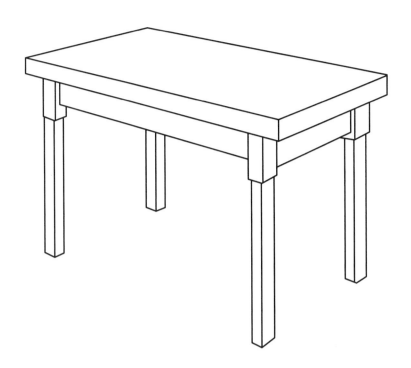

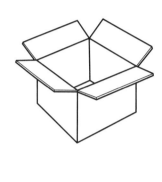

Draw a 🌙 above the box.

Draw a ◯ in the box.

Draw a △ between the table and the box.

Draw a ♡ near the box.

Draw a ☺ under the table.

Draw a ☐ on the table.

Draw a ☆ to the left of the table.

Is the box to the right or the left of the table? _____

# Data Analysis and Probability

**Materials:**
- Paper or plastic bags
- Linking cubes
- Crayons or colored pencils
- Pattern blocks
- Colored chips
- 1/2-inch graph paper
- Activity sheets (pages 83–85)

## Objective

Sort and graph a collection of objects and analyze the data.

## Mini-Lesson

1. Before the lesson, write a list of 4 to 5 objects commonly found outside the school (for example, twig, small rock, leaf, and pinecone). Make 1 copy of the list for every 2 to 3 students.
2. Take the class outside for a short nature scavenger hunt. Divide students into groups of 2 or 3. Give each group a bag and the list of objects to find.
3. Have students search for as many of each object as they can find and place them in their bags, allowing only 3 minutes for students to do so.
4. Return to the classroom. Have students work together to sort the collected objects on the floor or the table and arrange the objects in columns, similar to a pictograph.
5. Ask questions about the graph. For example, "Did you find more rocks or more leaves?"

## Group 1 ○

**Linking Cubes Graph**

1. Give each student a set of linking cubes (2 yellow, 5 blue, and 8 red), a sheet of graph paper, and crayons or colored pencils.
2. Have students sort their cubes by color and link them together. When placed on the table side by side, the linking cubes should resemble a bar graph. Do this step with your own set of linking cubes as well.
3. Ask questions based on students' linking cube graphs. For example, "What color are most of the cubes? How many blue cubes are there?"
4. Show students how to arrange the linked cubes to compare the heights of the "bars" and to easily compare and answer questions about the number of each color.

## Group 2 ☐

**Bar Graph**

1. Select 20 pattern blocks of 4 different shapes and place them in the center of the group.
2. Have students work together to sort the blocks by shape and arrange them in columns, similar to a pictograph. Show students how 3 larger shapes may make a taller column than 5 smaller shapes. Ask, "Do the heights of the columns of shapes relate to the number of shapes? How could we arrange them so that they do?"
3. Give each student a sheet of graph paper to create a bar graph to reflect the results of the block sort. Show students how to label and align their graphs.
4. Ask questions based on the graphs such as, "What shape has the least number of blocks? What 2 shapes have the same number of blocks? How can you tell?"

## Group 3 △

**Tally and Graph**

1. Give each student 30 chips in 5 different colors, a sheet of graph paper, and crayons or colored pencils.
2. Help students make tally charts of the 5 colors. Then, have students sort their chips by color, making a tally mark beside each color as they count and sort the chips.
3. Show students how to create graphs with labels for each color along the bottoms and numbers along the left sides.
4. Have students transfer the information from their tally charts onto their bar graphs.
5. Ask questions based on the graphs. For example, "What color on your graph has the most chips?" Invite students to write their own questions and compare their graphs.

Name_____

Use linking cubes to make the graph shown. Line up the cubes with the picture. Use blue for the first column, red for the second column, and yellow for the third column.

## Colors of Linking Cubes

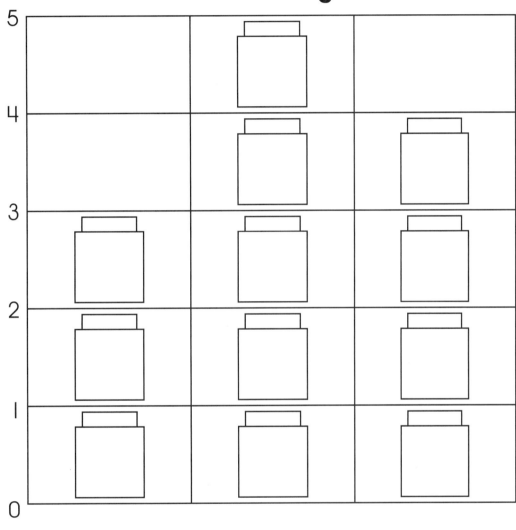

_____   _____   _____

How many cubes are in each column? Write the numbers on the lines.

Color the columns of cubes to match the linking cubes.

Which color of cubes are there the most of? _____

Which color of cubes are there the least of? _____

Name_____

How many are there of each fruit? Write the numbers on the lines.

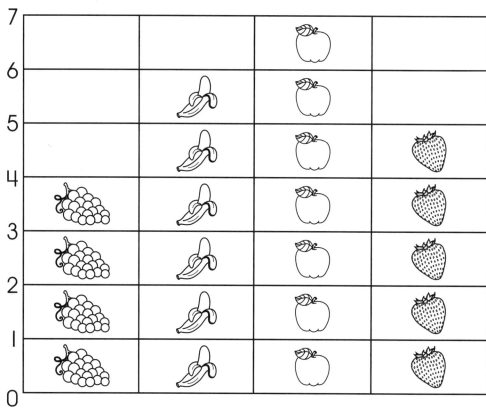

**Lunchtime Fruits**

_____   _____   _____   _____

Use the graph to answer the questions.

How many people had a  with lunch?_____

How many people had  with lunch? _____

Which fruit did the most people eat? _____

Which fruit did the fewest people eat? _____

How many more people ate a  than  ?_____

Name_____

Count the shape stickers. Use the tally chart to keep track of the totals. Use the tally chart to help you color the bar graph.

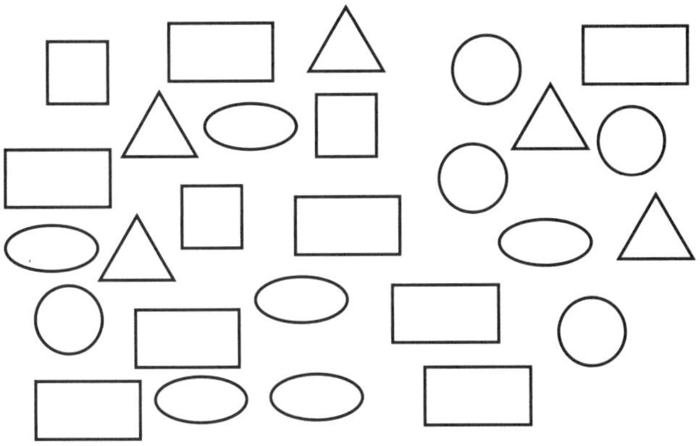

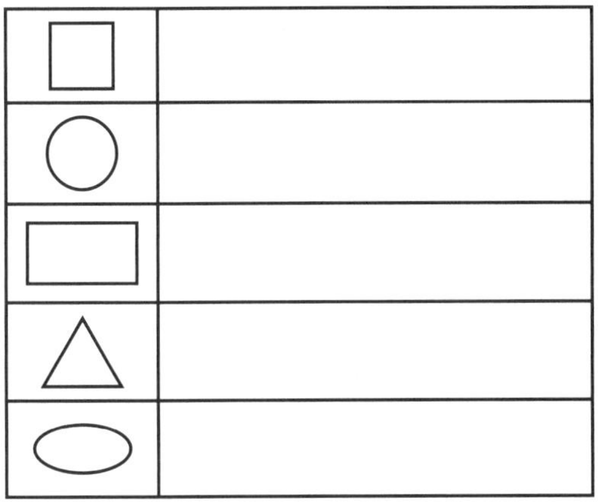

**Sticker Shapes**

**Tally Chart**

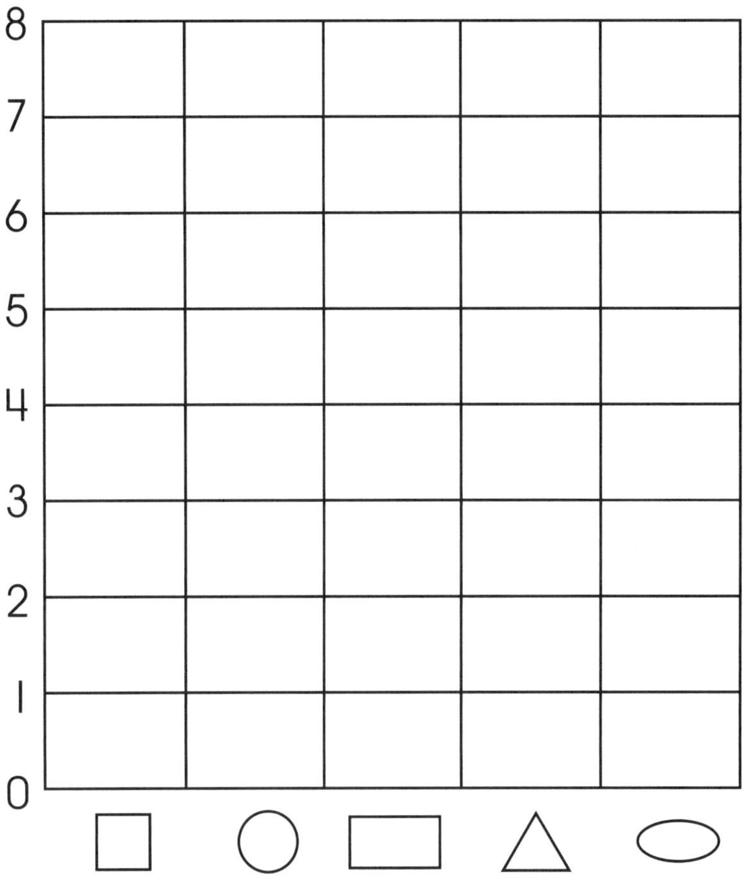

Use the bar graph to answer the questions.

Which 2 shapes have the same number of stickers? _____

Which shape has the most stickers? _____

Which shape has the least stickers? _____

How many more rectangle stickers are there than circle stickers?_____

# Data Analysis and Probability

**Materials:**
- Overhead projector
- 1/2-inch graph transparencies (2)
- 1/2-inch graph paper
- Pencils
- Index cards
- Picture cards (cat, dog, and fish) (1 of each per student)
- Activity sheets (pages 87–89)

## Objective
Ask a question, gather data, and display the results as a bar graph.

## Mini-Lesson

1. Place 1 of the graph transparencies on the overhead projector.
2. Write the title *Favorite Colors* at the top. Write the colors *red, blue, yellow,* and *green* on the x-axis. Number the y-axis 1 to 10.
3. Ask, "Which color do you like the best?" Survey the class and color a square in the appropriate column on the graph for each color selected. As you create the graph, think aloud through the process, making sure to use the terms *survey* and *bar graph*.
4. Once you complete the bar graph, ask questions based on the results of the survey. For example, "How many people liked red the best?"
5. Using a new transparency, repeat the process with a different survey question.

## Group 1 ○

**Yes-or-No Survey**
1. Give each student an index card with a red X on one side and a green check mark on the other.
2. Decide together what yes-or-no question you want to ask the group. For example, "Do you like chocolate—yes or no?"
3. Survey the group. As students share their answers, have them place their cards with the X side or the check mark side faceup on the table, lining up all of the X's in one column and all of the check marks in another column.
4. Give students graph paper and pencils and help them draw simple bar graphs to show the results. Once students complete the graphs, discuss the results.
5. If time allows, repeat the activity with a new survey question.

## Group 2 □

**Favorites Survey**
1. Give each student a sheet of graph paper, a pencil, and 1 of each animal card (cat, dog, and fish).
2. Ask, "Which of these pets do you like best—cat, dog, or fish?"
3. Work together to create a pictograph. Have each student select the animal he likes best and place the card on the table in the appropriate place.
4. Guide students through the process of creating bar graphs to reflect the results of the survey. Discuss the results.
5. Ask, "How did having just 3 choices help us organize and use the data we collected? What would have happened if our survey question did not give choices?"
6. Challenge students to practice writing their own survey questions and, if possible, gather and display the data on a bar graph.

## Group 3 △

**Statistical Survey**
1. Discuss how all kinds of information is collected about people and used for everything from deciding where to build new schools to what products to sell at grocery stores.
2. Brainstorm information that can be collected about students at their school (for example, age, number of siblings, transportation, etc.)
3. Have students choose a topic and write a survey question to ask the group. Remind students to offer specific choices.
4. Give students graph paper and pencils and help them create bar graphs from their surveys.
5. Have students survey their classmates. Remind them to record each person's answer on their bar graphs.
6. Discuss the results of everyone's surveys. Ask questions that encourage students to compare items on their graphs and to think about how their statistical information could be useful for the class or the school.

Name_____

Think of a yes-or-no question that you would like to ask. Write it on the line.

My Question _____

Label the bar graph with a title, yes and no, and the number of people (0 to 5).

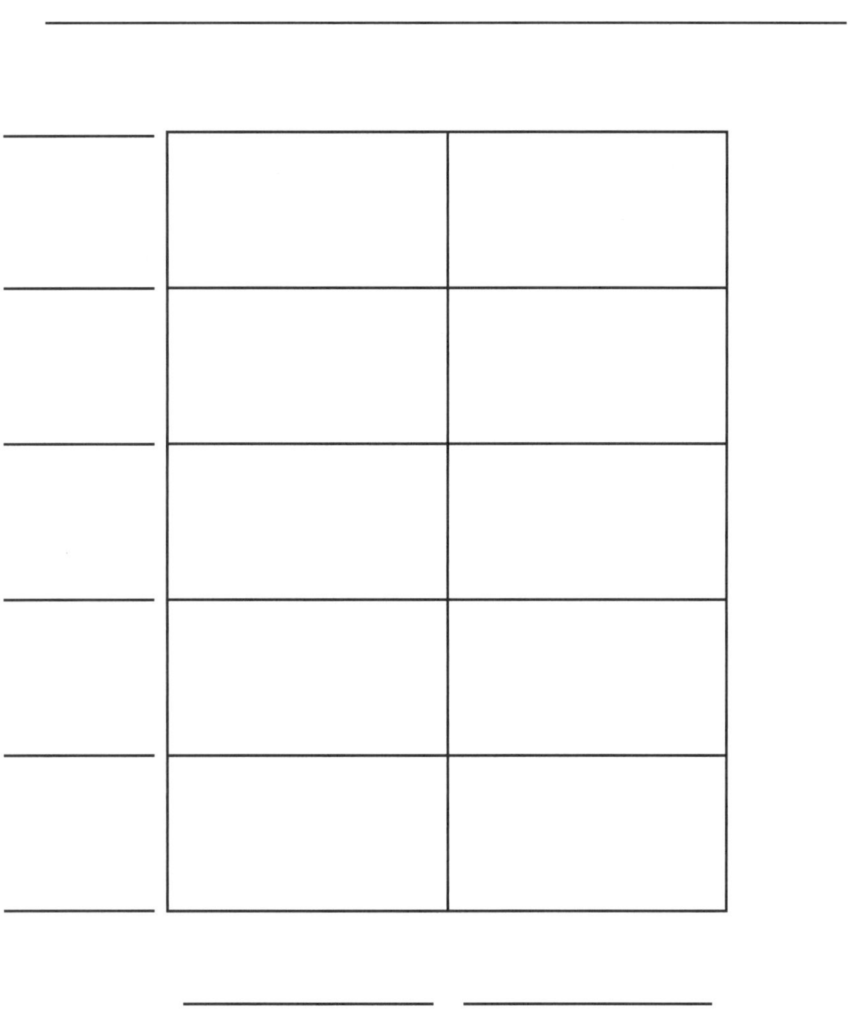

_____

_____   _____

_____

_____

_____

_____

_____   _____

Survey 5 people. Show their answers on the bar graph. Answer the questions.

Which answer did the most people give? _____

Which answer did the fewest people give? _____

Name_____

Think of a 3-choice favorite question that you would like to ask. Write it on the line.

My Question _____

Label the bar graph with a title, the 3 choices, and the number of people (0 to 7).

_____

Survey 7 people. Show their answers on the bar graph. Answer the questions.

Which choice did the most people like? _____

Which choice did the fewest people like? _____

How many more people chose the favorite than the least favorite? _____

CD-104541 © Carson-Dellosa

Name_____

Think of a survey question that you would like to ask. Offer up to 4 choices. Write it on the line.

My Question _____

Label the bar graph with a title, the choices, and the number of people (0 to 12).

_____

Survey up to 12 people. Show their answers on the bar graph. Answer the questions.

Which answer did the most people give? _____

Which answer did the fewest people give? _____

Write a sentence explaining the results of your survey.

_____

# Data Analysis and Probability

**Materials:**
- Index cards
- Colored counting chips
- Opaque bag
- Spinners (real or pictures)
- Paper circles and crayons
- Chart paper
- Activity sheets (pages 91–93)

## Objective
Determine probability as likely, unlikely, or certain.

## Mini-Lesson

1. Give each student 3 index cards. Have students draw a smiley face on 1 card, a straight face on the second card, and a sad face on the third card.
2. Explain that the card with a smiley face means *certain,* the card with a straight face means *likely,* and the card with a sad face means *unlikely.* Discuss the meanings of the words and brainstorm scenarios for each.
3. Ask questions that can be answered with *likely, unlikely,* or *certain.* For example, if it were Friday, you might say, "Tomorrow will be Saturday." (certain) If it were the middle of May, you could say, "It will snow tomorrow." (unlikely)
4. For each situation, tell students to raise their cards of choice in the air. Stop to discuss when students have a difference of opinion.

## Group 1 ○

**Probability**

1. Place 4 counting chips of one color and 1 counting chip of a different color in an opaque bag (for example, 4 blue and 1 red).
2. Pull out a chip, show it to the group, and place it back in the bag. Repeat several times.
3. Ask, "Which color do you think I am most likely to pull from the bag? Why? Do you think more [blue] chips or [red] chips are the bag? Why?"
4. Display the chips on the table. Introduce the words *likely* and *unlikely* as they pertain to the activity. Repeat the activity with a different number or combination of chips.
5. Try placing all of the same color of chips in the bag and discuss the terms *certain* and *impossible.*

## Group 2 ☐

**Spinners**

1. Introduce spinners. Talk about how spinners work. Define likelihood as it pertains to spinners.
2. Draw a spinner on chart paper and color the entire spinner blue. Ask, "How likely is it that I will land on blue?" (certain) Encourage students to explain why.
3. Draw another spinner that is about 3/4 red and 1/4 yellow. Ask students to identify the likelihood of landing on red (likely) and yellow (unlikely). Challenge students to explain why the answer would not be *certain* for either of the colors. Then, ask the likelihood of landing on blue (impossible).
4. Distribute paper circles and crayons. Have students create 4 spinners where the likelihood of landing on green is *certain, likely, unlikely,* and *impossible.* Ask students to explain the thought process behind each of their spinners.

## Group 3 △

**Fair or Unfair?**

1. Children care about *fair* and *unfair.* Draw a spinner on chart paper and color the entire spinner orange. Say, "Let's pretend we are playing a game. Any time the spinner lands on blue, it is your turn. Any time the spinner lands on orange, it is my turn." Students will surely point out that the game is unfair.
2. Discuss *likely, unlikely, certain,* and *impossible* as they relate to fair and unfair spinners. Ask, "For a spinner to be fair for both players, how could we describe the likelihood of landing on each color?" (equally likely)
3. Distribute paper and crayons. Have students create fair and unfair spinners for 2 players and for 4 players. Have students explain their thinking as they work.
4. Have students share their spinners and ask other students to identify red as *likely, unlikely, certain,* or *impossible.*

CD-104541 © Carson-Dellosa

Name_____

For each spinner, is it likely that you will spin a 2? Circle *yes* or *no*.

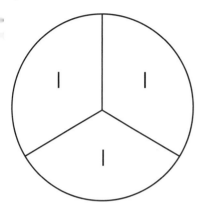

yes          no

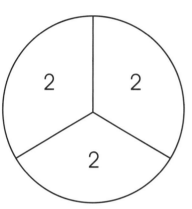

yes          no

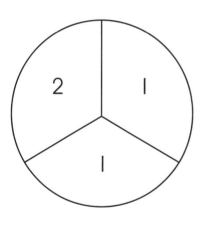

yes          no

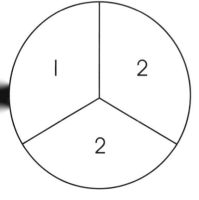

yes          no

Name_____

For each spinner, what is the likelihood of spinning a 2? Circle your answers.

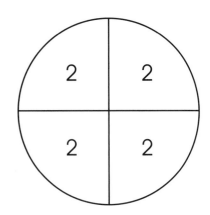

certain    likely    unlikely

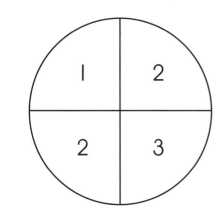

certain    likely    unlikely

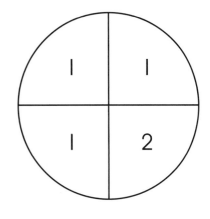

certain    likely    unlikely

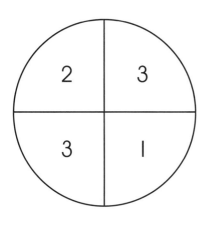

certain    likely    unlikely

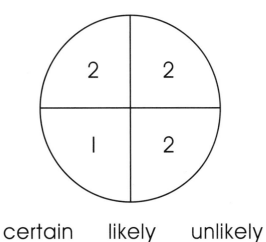

certain    likely    unlikely

certain    likely    unlikely

Name_____

You will need at least 4 crayons. Create a fair spinner for . . .

2 players

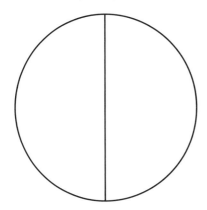

3 players

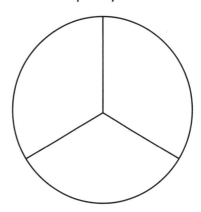

4 players

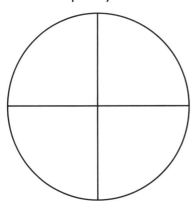

3 players

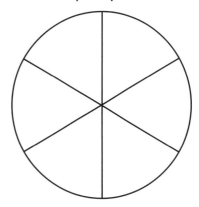

2 players

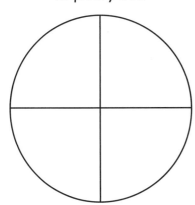

4 players

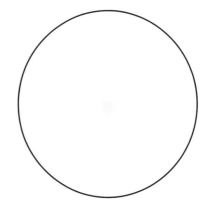

# Answer Key

**Page 7**

1; 3; 6; 2; 5; 4; 7

**Page 8**

(across each row) 4; 7; 7; 9; 9; 4; Matching sets should be colored the same color.

**Page 9**

3; 8; 9; 8; Answers will vary. Answers will vary.

**Page 11**

More–5; Less–2; More–4; Less–1; 5 dogs; 1 cat; 3 more kids

**Page 12**

More–6; Less–5; Answers will vary. Answers will vary. 6 more kids

**Page 13**

4; less; 1; 10 circles; Less/More– Answers will vary; 2 and 3; 10 and 9

**Page 15**

bird; first girl; triangle; students will color the 2nd smiley face yellow; 1st

**Page 16**

circle–frog; square–fish; oval–red; triangle–blue; 3rd and 8th; triangle, circle, rectangle, square, oval

**Page 17**

MATH IS FUN! A BUTTERFLY

**Page 19**

3; 4; 4; 5; 6; 6; 7; Answers will vary but may include 1 + 6 or 2 + 5.

**Page 20**

3 + 3 = 6; 4 + 5 = 9; 6 + 2 = 8; Answers will vary but may include 1 + 9, 2 + 8, 3 + 7, 4 + 6, or 5 + 5.

**Page 21**

3, 2 + 1 = 3; 5, 1 + 4 = 5; 9, 6 + 3 = 9; 10, 5 + 5 = 10; 9, 7 + 2 = 9; 10, 4 + 6 = 10; 8, 0 + 8 = 8

**Page 23**

1; 5; 2; 4; 1; 2; 0

**Page 24**

8; X on 2 apples; 9; X on 1 apple; 7; X on 3 apples; 4; X on 6 apples; 6; X on 4 apples

**Page 25**

2; 3; 8; 0; 6; 3; 5; 7 − 2 = 5; 3; 5 − 3 = 2

**Page 27**

2, 4, 6, 8, and 10 yellow; 5, 10, 15, and 20 blue; 10, 20, 30, 40, and 50 green

**Page 28**

10, 12, 14, 16, 18, 20; 20, 25, 30, 35, 40, 45, 50; 50, 60, 70, 80, 90, 100; 2, 4, 6, 8, 10, 12, 14, 16, 18, 20; Answers will vary.

**Page 29**

2, 4, 6, 8, 10, 12, 14, 16, 18, 20; 5, 10, 15, 20, 25, 30, 35; 10, 20, 30, 40, 50, 60

**Page 31**

1|1; 2|2; 3|3; 4|4; 5|5

**Page 32**

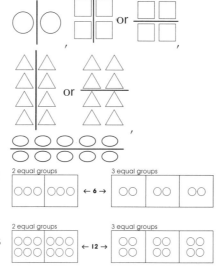

**Page 33**

5 – no, no, no; 6 – yes, yes, no; 7 – no, no, no; 8 – yes, no, yes; 9 – no, yes, no; 10 – yes, no, no; 11 – no, no, no; 12 – yes, yes, yes; 13 – no, no, no; 14 – yes, no, no; 15 – no, yes, no

**Page 35**

1; 3; 8; 10; 12

**Page 36**

**Page 37**

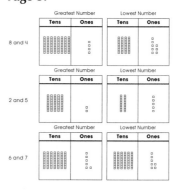

**Page 39**

Answers will vary. X on the square; X on the equilateral triangle (bottom left); X on the cat; X on the sad face; X on the square with a bigger dot; X on the carrot

**Page 40**

Answers will vary.

**Page 41**

By 2s–2, 4, 6, 8, 12, 14, 16, 18, 22, 24; By 5s–5, 15, 25; Both–10, 20; Outside–1, 3, 7, 9, 11, 13, 17, 19, 21, 23. X on the 6; X on the 3; X on the 62; X on the 1

**Page 43**

red, blue; yellow, green; black, white, blue; green, green, purple; red, yellow, yellow

**Page 44**

square, circle, triangle; circle, square, square; Answers will vary. Pattern should be AB. Pattern should be AAB.

# Answer Key

**Page 45**

Answers will vary.

**Page 47**

yes; no; no; yes; 4 triangles; 7 squares

**Page 48**

yes; no; 4 circles; 8 stacked smiley faces; 8; 7; 10

**Page 49**

8-unit tall rectangle, 10-unit tall rectangle; 2-unit long rectangle, 1-unit long rectangle; 5, 6; 6, 4; 20, 25; 10, 0; Answers will vary. Answers will vary.

**Page 51**

square; rectangle; striped square, white square; circle, square, circle; down arrow, down arrow, up arrow

**Page 52**

B, E; J, N, P; U, V, X, Y; Z, W, U; 4, 6; 5, 8, 10; 6, 10; 14, 13, 10

**Page 53**

(by row) 8, 10, 11; 4, 6, 12, 14; 15, 5; +2; +2; –10

**Page 55**

pencil; envelope; soccer ball; backpack; crayon; teaspoon; crayon; straw

**Page 56**

2, 1, 3; 1, 3, 2; 2 paper clips; 5 paper clips; 4 paper clips; A; B

**Page 57**

2, 4, 1, 3; 6 small paper clips, 3–4 large paper clips; 3 small paper clips, 2 large paper clips; 4 small paper clips, 3 large paper clips; B; A; Answers will vary.

**Page 59**

drinking glass; full-size pool; 1/2-Liter water bottle; can of soup; glass and can

**Page 60**

3, 2, 1; 2, 1, 3; 1, 3, 2; glass and can

**Page 61**

4, 1, 2, 3; can of soup; cup; gallon; quart; pint

**Page 63**

2, 4, 1, 3; May; 31; Monday; 5; Tuesday

**Page 64**

7, 2, 5, 3, 4, 6, 1; April; 30; 5; Thursday; Friday, 10; Wednesday, 3

**Page 65**

7, 2, 5, 3, 4, 6, 1; 4, 1, 9, 11, 6, 3, 10, 12, 5, 2, 8, 7; February; 28; Sunday, 14; 8; Friday; January

**Page 67**

yellow–reading, eating, brushing teeth; blue–sleeping, school, playing soccer; Answers will vary.

**Page 68**

yellow–going to school, waking up; red–playing, eating lunch; green–eating dinner; blue sleeping; Answers will vary.

**Page 69**

(top row) 3, 5, 8, 2; (bottom row) 7, 1, 6, 4; (bottom-left column) G, D, B, H; (bottom-right column) F, C, E, A

**Page 71**

Check students' answers.

**Page 72**

Check students' answers.

**Page 73**

Check students' answers.

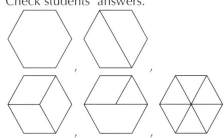

answers will vary.

**Page 75**

(by row) 4, 8, 4; 3, 0, 4; 4, 6, 5; 4, 3, 0; 4, 3, 3

**Page 76**

octagon; square; oval; pentagon; triangle; hexagon; circle; rectangle

**Page 77**

Answers will vary.

**Page 79**

(left column) between 6; far 4; in 2; (right column) near 3; on 1; under 5; square; rectangle; circle

**Page 80**

under; answers will vary.

**Page 81**

right

**Page 83**

3; 5; 4; Cubes should be colored correctly; red; blue

**Page 84**

4; 6; 7; 5; 6; 5; apples; grapes; 2 more people

# Answer Key

## Page 85

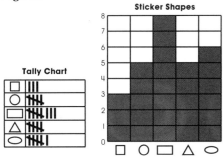

circle and triangle; rectangle; square; 3 more rectangle stickers

## Page 87

Questions, surveys, and graphs will vary. (y-axis) 5, 4, 3, 2, 1, 0; (x-axis) yes, no; Answers will vary.

## Page 88

Questions, surveys, and graphs will vary. (y-axis) 7, 6, 5, 4, 3, 2, 1, 0; (x-axis) Labels will vary. Answers will vary.

## Page 89

Questions, surveys, and graphs will vary. (y-axis) 12, 11, 10, 9, 8, 7, 6, 5, 4, 3, 2, 1, 0; (x-axis) Labels will vary. Answers will vary.

## Page 91

no; yes; no; yes

## Page 92

certain; likely; unlikely; unlikely; likely; unlikely

## Page 93

Halves colored differently; Thirds colored differently; Fourths colored differently; Thirds colored differently; Halves colored differently; Fourths colored differently.